Lake Huron Summer Dance Pavilions

Sand, Surf and Music

by Peter Young

Published by: PDA Communications Ltd.
                  76 Hillcroft Street
                  Oshawa, Ontario, Canada
                  L1G 2L2

CANADIAN CATALOGUING IN PUBLICATION DATA

Young, Peter, 1949 -
        Lake Huron's Summer Dance Pavilions

Includes Index.
ISBN 0-9681951-1-3

1. Pavilions - Ontario - Huron, Lake, Region - History.
2. Dance parties - Ontario - Huron, Lake, Region - History.
3. Dance orchestras - Ontario - Huron, Lake, Region - History.
4. Huron, Lake, Region (Mich. And Ont.) - History. I. Title.

FC3095.H87Y68 1998   971.3'2   C98-930841-3
F1059.H95Y68 1998

To my wife Debra

THE PAVILION

Dancing at the Pavilion is always associated with happiness. No matter what the style of music, its infectious rhythm calls people together, to start moving, to dance, to have fun. People meet people; friendships are made; some fall in love. The love-songs the hands play become a very personal thing to lovers. The chord changes, the lyrics, the melody all reach the inner soul and the song becomes "our song." The words may change, but the feeling is always deep, true and enduring.

So another summer at the Pavilion brings exciting groups to provide happy music for you to enjoy, to dance and to make friends.

(reprinted from a 1972 Sauble Beach Pavilion events poster)

COME DANCING

(words & music by Ray Davies, Davray Music Ltd.)

They put a parking lot on a piece of land
Where the supermarket used to stand
Before that they put up a bowling alley
On the site that used to be the local Palais
That's where the big bands used to come and play
My sister went there on a Saturday.

Come Dancing
All her boyfriends used to come and call
Why not Come Dancing
It's only natural.

Another Saturday another date
She would be ready but she'd always make him wait
In the hallway in anticipation
He didn't know the night would end up in frustration
He'd end up blowing all his wages for the week
All for a cuddle and the peck on the cheek.

Come Dancing
That's how they did it when I was just a kid
And when you said Come Dancing
My sister always did.

The day they knocked down the Palais
My sister stood and cried
The day they knocked down the Palais
Part of her childhood died - just died....

Come Dancing
Just like The Palais on a Saturday
And all her friends would Come Dancing
Where the big bands used to play.

Table Of Contents

Preface

Preface

As the words in 'The Pavilion' remind us, people who danced at any of Lake Huron's memorable pavilions will likely look back on those times with great happiness.

There was a time in Ontario when the May 24th long weekend was the traditional opening date for most of Ontario's dance pavilions. During this annual salute to summer's pending arrival, wooden shutters would be raised, the dance floor was lovingly polished until it gleamed in preparation for another season of dancing feet, the refreshment booth was stocked up and posters were distributed throughout cottage country announcing the season's attractions.

Summer romances, moonlight strolls along Huron's clean sandy beaches, the unforgettable music of our youth (Big Band, Rock or Country & Western), hot cars and lasting friendships were all packed into two short months. There was so much fun to cram into July and August when the days were long and warm and the evening breezes were gentle. Up and down the shore of Lake Huron music soared from the beachfront dance halls and beckoned us.

And we responded to the call. Practically every night of the week there was a dance happening within driving distance of your home or cottage, and we filled those pavilions. Whether you swayed to the mellow sounds of the Big Bands, or rocked and rolled to some of Ontario's best rock groups, dancing was the highlight of people's summers for well over 50 years at some locations.

When I initially began researching Ontario's dance pavilions, I soon realized that this was a subject that touched people's hearts in a very significant manner. Regardless of a person's age or occupation, the youthful memories they cherish of their favourite dance pavilion bring on a smile as they fondly recollect some special moment. Dancing, music and the good times they gave us is one common denominator we all seem to share.

To chronicle Lake Huron's dance pavilions in a dry,

factual manner would be a great injustice to these wonderful halls. They were places of entertainment injected with a special life by the individual owners, the musicians and of course, those of us who came to dance. In this book I have tried to recognize many of the people who devoted a good portion of their career providing places of enjoyment for their customers. I've also made an effort to at least mention some of the hundreds of the individual musicians along with the orchestras and bands they led, who considered a gig at one of the pavilions more than a job - it was a holiday as well. And by including anecdotes from many people, I hope you will perhaps recall your own special moment from a past summer.

In May, 1997, I published my first book on the subject of Ontario's dance pavilions. Entitled 'The Kee To Bala Is Dunn's Pavilion,' this work brought back many good memories for people who danced at Muskoka's great lakeside hall (which continues to operate to this day). My intention was to follow this book with a much larger edition on the broad subject of Ontario's dance halls, but I decided instead to concentrate on another specific geographic area - Lake Huron - which has enabled me to include much more information and visual material about this area of the province than would be possible in a larger project.

We begin our dance hall tour near Owen Sound at the Balmy Beach Pavilion, which from a quick glance at a map is obviously not on Lake Huron. But since this hall was such an integral part of the summer entertainment circuit, I decided to stretch the parameters just a bit to include Balmy Beach. After travelling up to the hamlet of Oliphant we then head south on Highway 21 which hugs the Lake Huron coast, stopping off at a dozen more places along the 250+ kilometre route, winding up in Sarnia.

You'll find more in-depth coverage on certain pavilions than on others, but that's simply because I was able to discover more information about these places during my research - the length of each chapter does not necessarily reflect upon the significance or importance of the halls to people. I do hope that you'll learn something new about your favourite Huron hall, and also enjoy reading about some of the places that perhaps you knew about, but did not visit.

I would like to express my heartfelt thanks to so many people who granted interviews, sent letters and shared photographs and other material with me. There are many quotes from these folks throughout the text, and all photographs are credited at the back of the book. I should also mention that most of the material in this book has been obtained through interviews and letters, since very little information is available from published sources. In some cases many years have passed, which could influence the contributor's precise recollection of events. However, everyone with whom I spoke or corresponded has sincerely attempted to his or her best ability to relate their experiences as accurately as possible. (Since much of the research took place during 1995, naturally certain circumstances may have altered. Quotes from interviews and letters are usually attributed to the speaker or writer in the present tense, for the sake of continuity.)

So put on your dancing shoes and come join me as we fire up your favourite set of wheels, crank up the tape deck and take off for an adventure along Highway 21 to visit Lake Huron's Dance Pavilions.

Oshawa
February 1998

.

Chapter One

OWEN SOUND - BALMY BEACH DANCE PAVILION

Many an adjective has been used to describe dance floors in various pavilions around Ontario - "the best dance floor in the area," "the smoothest dance floor on the lake," "the largest dance floor in eastern (or western or northern or southern) Ontario," ... you may have your own words that best portray your favourite floor. Some halls even boasted they featured the best or the biggest dance floor in Canada.

The Balmy Beach Dance Pavilion four miles north of Owen Sound falls into this latter category and was quite proud to be able to make the claim that it had one of the largest dance floors in Canada. Not just in Ontario - in Canada.

This fact may never be proven, but with measurements of 106 by 140 feet, its 15,000 square feet of dancing space certainly gave it the distinction as having **one** of the largest floors in the country.

Balmy Beach was much more than a large dance pavilion. For more than 30 years this hall, owned by Joseph K. McLauchlan, was the centre of social activity for people from the Owen Sound district as well as for those who travelled to Grey/Bruce County for their vacations. The pavilion was set in the beautiful surroundings of McLauchlan Park where people could swim, picnic or stay in the Balmy Beach Lodge.

The park itself has an interesting history. It was established in 1898 when Joseph's brother, John H. McLauchlan, purchased 70 acres of land at Balmy Beach and erected a large pavilion and bandstand. The official opening was July 1, 1899. Initially one small ferry boat named *Lillie* brought visitors to the park's wharf, but the park was such a hit that John immediately purchased an additional boat, the *Mazeppa*, followed by an even larger vessel, *Canada* which operated until 1908.

In an article describing Dominion Day, 1899, Owen Sound Library Director Andrew Armitage expands on the entrepreneur John McLauchlan. "He was a man of vision. In one short year he had turned his new property into a wonderland resort. Jack, as he was known in the community, was going to put Owen Sound on the tourist map once and for all. His dream was to rival anything that could be found in the Muskokas. There was to be a large pavilion, a theatre, sporting fields and a long dock. Concerts and plays in the theatre would enrich the cultural life of visitors. Cottage lots were available at reasonable rates. Balmy Beach was to become the most fashionable of weekend retreats."

Hopes were so high for the park that The Georgian Bay Park and Summer Resort Company was formed to build a large summer hotel and purchased land from Jack to carry out its plans. In 1902, one of the most impressive buildings ever constructed in the area opened its doors - the King's Royal Hotel, with a capacity for 200 guests and its own hydro system. The cost: $90,000.

Sadly, the optimistic plans for developing a major resort gradually fell apart; the hotel lost money from Day One, taking the company into liquidation. After only 12 years of operation the hotel's hydro was turned off forever, and the building was demolished two years later. In a 1962 interview, Joseph McLauchlan told the local newspaper that insurance companies would not cover hotels at this time, due to the high risk of fire.

About ten years after the hotel's demise, the original pavilion was moved and converted into the Balmy Beach Lodge. At this time, Joseph McLauchlan was running the family park and decided to dismantle the theatre, move it as well, and open the Balmy Beach Dance Pavilion. Much of the material that was once the theatre was used in the transformation of the building.

Joseph's granddaughter, Gayle, writes about the new dance pavilion. "When they say the theatre and pavilion were 'moved,' my guess is that it was less than a block. The

Balmy Beach New Dance Pavilion

lodge was opened in 1929 and the pavilion shortly afterwards. Although I didn't attend dances there, I can remember being in the dance hall regularly with my grandfather, but it was closed up and boarded by then."

One person who does remember the Balmy Beach Dance Pavilion very well is Ken Bowes. He writes: "I played trumpet with the Lloyd Kibbler Band during the 1950's. During the summers we played at Balmy Beach, at Sauble Beach Pavilion and also the Port Elgin Casino on Lake Huron. The Balmy Beach Dance Pavilion had the recognition of the best dance floor in Ontario during the late 1940's and 50's. I can recall advance sale of tickets for Balmy Beach Saturday night dancing - all tickets were sold prior to five o'clock that afternoon. This pavilion enjoyed great respect during the years it operated. The young of today will not enjoy the times we had at these places as most no longer exist, which is very unfortunate."

Vicki Storm grew up in Owen Sound. "I have wonderful memories of the dance pavilions and big bands within driving distance of Owen Sound in the 1940's and 50's," she writes. "The greatest dance pavilion of all time was Balmy Beach Pavilion where Lloyd Kibbler's orchestra played. The best jazz dancers travelled to many of these halls. Two of the best dancers in Owen Sound were Lloyd Kibbler's son and Colleen Bowman. I also went to Sauble Beach Pavilion where every Wednesday night the Ranch Boys played and Saturday nights featured big bands. Kincardine, Hanover, Port Elgin, Wasaga Beach's Dardanella … I travelled to them all. What wonderful times!"

The Balmy Beach Dance Pavilion, the last building left standing in McLauchlan Park, was demolished in June 1962. Lumber from the dismantled building, including the largest dance floor in Canada, was sold at a general auction.

Chapter Two

OLIPHANT - McKENZIE'S PAVILION

If you happen to be familiar with the hamlets and towns in the Bruce Peninsula area of the province, chances are you may have heard of the little community of Oliphant. Located on the Lake Huron side of the Bruce, it is primarily a cottage region with only a handful of year-round residents who remain to brave the icy winter as its blasts across the open water.

But during the gentle summer months of July and August, Oliphant is home to many people who have cottages either along the beach, or out on the islands which are just a short boat ride from shore. Although a number of newer cottages have been built in Oliphant in recent years, many residents are proud to be second and third generation "Oliphant stock," of both the seasonal and permanent variety.

Perhaps one of the most well-known of these families is that of William 'Mac' McKenzie. It was Mac's grandfather, Murdock, along with Mac's father William, and uncle Thomas, who built McKenzie's Pavilion back in 1921.

Murdock owned the farm nearest to the beach, and in the beginning built a small store adjacent to his farm home to provide supplies to the first island cottagers. He also established the first post office around 1904. Along with waiting for the mail to arrive, bonfires in the evenings were the only other form of socializing. As Mac writes, "In the late 1890's and early 1900's the first campers arrived in Oliphant by stage from the Wiarton railhead, and there was little to do except fish, canoe and row ashore from the islands to pick up supplies and mail." The first Oliphant Regatta took place in 1898 as a general picnic, and with the exception of two years during World War One, this event has been an annual affair.

Mac explains how the pavilion concept took shape. "When my father came back home from the First War after serving in the trenches of France and Germany, he suggested to Grandfather Murdock and his brother Tom that a dance operation might be a good idea. McKenzie's Pavilion was born."

The purpose of the building was twofold - the lower level was constructed so that island cottagers could park their automobiles in covered stalls, while a sizeable dance floor was built upstairs with British Columbia fir. During the winter people could store their boats downstairs in protected surroundings. In later years part of this area was converted into an ice house to store blocks of ice cut from the lake for the use of cottagers during the summer.

McKenzie's Pavilion is now called The Oliphant Pavilion.

Mac was born in 1927 and lived in the family home on the hill, just before the highway descends to Oliphant beach. He continues, "From a very early age - five or six - I would drift off to sleep three times weekly in the summer to the sounds of the orchestra wafting into the firefly-filled night on the shore. My older cousins 'took tickets,' and someday I knew that I would be able to stay up and do the same.

"You see, in those days, admission was ten cents per person to get in and five cents for every dance. A dance at our pavilion consisted of two musical numbers. Patrons were behind a railing where seats were available along three sides, and there were two entrances to the floor."

During the '30's and '40's McKenzie's Pavilion attracted dancers from up and down the Lake Huron and Georgian Bay shores of the Bruce, including people from the city of Owen Sound, more than twenty miles away.

Mac elaborates on his recollections of working in the dance hall. "So, our job - brother Don and myself, dressed in white short pants and blue blazers made by my mother - was to take the tickets as couples entered the floor and to make certain that all left after the second dance. Tickets, as I mentioned, were five cents each or six for a quarter. I remember one Torontonian who served as an example to me from a financial point of view. He would buy just one ticket at a time for five cents, after deciding that he and his date would have the next dance. Even though the tickets were good all season, and could have been used the following week or for the next dance night, he stuck to his single ticket purchases. He eventually became treasurer of one of Toronto's largest advertising agencies!"

Some of the orchestras playing at McKenzie's Pavilion in the 1920's, 1930's and 1940's included Earl Gate and Harry Parker from Owen Sound, Bert Raynor of Southampton, and Arch Barnard from Wiarton. Individual music stars like Eb Smith, John Gould (who later became a famous Canadian artist) and Len George were only a few of the many talented individuals who entertained there.

The building was initially lit by a thirty-two volt Delco system which provided the only electric lights in Oliphant; Ontario Hydro did not reach the area until the late 1940's. Since the band could not use amplifiers or microphones at this time, vocalists used a galvanized conical shaped megaphone and this helped to project the voice over the floor. Mac says an American, Bill Sanderson of the Buffalo area, would create no end of longing looks from many of the women in the audience with his rendition of 'I Love You Truly.'

Getting the dance floor in shape was a major task, according to Mac. "First it had to be washed with strong soap and water. Then, paste wax (Johnson's Paste Wax) was applied by us to the whole floor on our hands and knees. Afterwards we had to polish the surface, pushing the twenty-five pound polisher with a soft woollen cloth attached. The morning after every dance, we swept the pavilion. During this 'sweeping detail' we carefully looked under all the seat cushions and benches for any nickel, dime or sometimes (Wow!) quarter that might have slipped or dropped out of some dancer's pocket the night before. The occasional lady's purse or lipstick would, of course, be returned to the owner or placed in a prominent place in the ticket booth for the next dance. And just before every dance night got under way, powdered wax was laid down for the dancers' feet to smooth into the surface."

Apparently Prime Minister Mackenzie King and Finance Minister James Malcom one time journeyed from Wiarton by stage to dance at McKenzie's Pavilion, followed by a late night snack at the Gideon Kastner cottage.

John Rutherford has fond memories of McKenzie's Pavilion in Oliphant. He was eighteen years old in 1946 when he decided to take one last long summer holiday before entering the world of work.

He writes, "A newspaper ad caught my eye, promising a two-month vacation at a summer cottage in Oliphant (wherever that was) in exchange for light duties. Not overly fond of hard work, I jumped at this opportunity, and boarded a train for Wiarton. I was met at the Wiarton station by my employer, Mr. Slee (a charming gentleman with two charming daughters), who drove me to his cottage in Oliphant.

"Oliphant in those days consisted of a mile of cottages facing the water, one General Store, a small frame church, a one-room schoolhouse and a huge barn-like structure called the Dance Pavilion. At the top of a tall flight of wooden stairs was a dance floor surrounded on three sides by a walk-way with benches, and a stage at the south-west corner.

"Throughout that glorious summer, dance bands came every Wednesday and Saturday evening and played for our dancing and listening pleasure. Much to my surprise there was a ritual about those evenings. Although most of the customers arrived on time (about 7:30 p.m.), no one seemed anxious to be first on the dance floor, watched, of course, by a hundred eyes peering out from three sides of that vast shadowy emptiness. Many an hour I spent warming one of those wooden benches, trying desperately to look at ease, and wondering whether 'now' was the right time to present myself to some shy beauty.

"During Intermission, the band's pianist played waltzes, which were not very popular, and it was only after this interlude that the dance floor came to life. But as the summer wore on, people became friendlier and many a match was made - and many a heart was broken.

"For the next four summers I returned to Oliphant, both as a visitor, and at the beginning of my teaching career to teach in the one-room schoolhouse. Then came the need to earn a living, the winds of life changed my course, and I never saw Oliphant again."

Mac recalls a very amusing incident which might go down in pavilion history as the only time dancers ever went on strike:

"One night during the early War years of the '40's the large crowd got the idea that the orchestra, Earl 'Swing' Gates and his Owen Sound band, were shortening the musical numbers in order to get in more dances and the resulting increase in income. Not true, but the crowd thought so. Soooooo, they decided to stage a sit-down strike - gals with fine gowns and men in blazers and grey pants, some with two-tone white and brown shoes, did just that. They sat down on the dance floor. The orchestra looked at the seated dancers. The dancers looked back. It was a stalemate.

"My Uncle Tom, who was in the ticket booth that night, motioned me over. 'Billie,' he said, 'go and tell the orchestra to play "God Save the King!"' They did - and laughing, the dancers rose to their feet, stood at attention for the national anthem, and then walked off the floor. The strike was over and the dance continued!"

When Murdock passed away, Mac's father and uncle operated the business, along with the adjacent Maple Leaf General Store. In the early 1940's they dissolved the partnership, with William taking over the pavilion, and Thomas operating the store. Mac further explains the arrangement. "William built a small annex to the pavilion and called it Mac's Snacks where sandwiches and soft drinks were sold in the daytime and during dance nights. Patrons would come over after the dance for ham sandwiches (25 cents) and a coke (5 cents). In 1957 ownership passed to my brother Murdoch McKenzie, and in the 1980's the business was passed to Uncle Tom's granddaughter, Susie Morris, who operated the building as a small craft store and renamed the building The Oliphant Pavilion."

As the Sauble Beach Pavilion - just a few miles south of Oliphant - grew in popularity in the late 1940's and into the 1950's, McKenzie's crowds began to diminish. Mac says that gradually the pavilion was only used for the annual Civic Holiday Regatta dance, and then even that was phased out.

Sonny Drumm owns the building today and operates a flea market and ice cream/frozen yogurt stand during the summer months. He laid a large flagstone floor for the flea market portion - all stones were found in the area.

There is talk each year at the annual regatta of opening the pavilion again for dances, but it is likely just talk. The structure would not be permitted to open without extensive renovations and safety features being installed. Sonny took measures to increase the stability of the beams and posts, and put on a new roof.

Upstairs, Sonny uses the space for storing some of his flea market merchandise, but in the southwest corner stands the original stage, with a small railing in front of it. There is a lonely old piano sitting with broken keys and strings on this stage which many years ago was the platform for the bands.

The old piano optimistically awaits the next dance to begin – unfortunately the instrument poses a major challenge for the technician.

Mac remembers the piano. "It belonged to the pavilion where it spent the frigid winters in solitary splendour on the bandstand, while the Lake Huron blizzards howled outside. Come Spring, the snowdrifts melted, and then in late June the lonely cottages again would start to show signs of life. The piano tuner would arrive - the first sign that the season begins again.

"The upper floor is deserted now - dust and cobwebs - but when I drift off to sleep on a warm summer night in Oliphant, I can still hear the strains of 'Amapola,' 'Yours,' 'The White Cliffs of Dover,' 'Begin the Beguine' and 'Stardust.'"

John Rutherford also has his own thoughts about McKenzie's Pavilion in Oliphant. "Sometimes on a hot summer evening I wonder if a crowd is beginning to gather at the Pavilion to listen, and to dance. Do young lovers still meet there and are hearts still broken? Even from almost fifty years away, I can hear 'The Things We Did Last Summer' and 'Slow Boat To China,' played by bands whose names I have forgotten, from a time that was innocent in a world that was young.

"Or is it only the ghosts of Summers Past that sway gently in the shadows, watched by the eyes of vanished youth?"

Chapter Three

SAUBLE BEACH

Danceiro

The building in recent years has been used as a winter storage facility, flea market and even an auto body shop, but people who recall those few glorious years in the late 1960's and early 70's know there's a very interesting and much more exciting past to this site than its outward appearance would indicate.

Dancerio was a different type of "body shop" in the 1960's and early 70's.

Located a mile or so north of the Sauble Falls Provincial Park on the road leading to Wiarton, Stewart Wilson built himself a dance hall in 1967 and called it Danceiro. "I ran an auto garage and collision business in Toronto, but had been coming up to Sauble Beach for many years," he explains. "Even though the pavilion near Sauble's main drag was going strong, I felt that the north beach area could do with another dance pavilion." So Stewart set about acquiring the land and having the building laid out.

On the suggestion of a designer - Mr. Tite from Shallow Lake - Stewart called his business Danceiro, which he says is Spanish for dance hall, because the structure resembled a Spanish building - a one-story low structure with a flat roof. Wib Wright from Owen Sound was the builder. "The hall was laid out so that the complete floor was free of posts," says Stewart. In fact he says it was the largest hall in the area without posts. The dance floor itself was poured cement with a special coating so that dancers could easily move their feet as they rocked and rolled. The interior of the hall was panelled, with a Spanish motif throughout; tables surrounding the floor were covered with cloths and candles while the exposed ceiling beams were painted flat black.

Stewart opened his hall in 1967 and ran it until 1972. "I originally started with rock bands from Toronto, London and other cities in hopes of attracting the large summer population of teenagers from these cities who gathered at the beach. To make the business viable, I really needed this crowd from the cities - appealing to kids strictly from the local area would just not bring in enough numbers."

Many name rock bands did play here, including the Calgary Stampeders, later known as The Stampeders who released a number of hit songs.

Singer Geoff Hewittson exhibits painful acrobatics at Danceiro in 1967. (He made a full recovery.)

Stewart worked through the week in Toronto, and travelled up to the beach and ran the dance hall on weekends. Sunday was clean-up day, and then it was back to the city for another week at the garage.

"One of the biggest challenges in providing entertainment for any age group is trying to gauge what the customers want. I tried appealing to the psychedelic tastes of the crowd, but found that after a couple of years of using rock bands, I was better off changing to a policy of hiring local bands which played a more versatile style of music." An older crowd began to attend, enjoying the variety of music which included country. But, as in many cases, without a liquor licence and the lower drinking age which the government introduced in the early 1970's, the competition with bars made it hard to attract a large enough crowd to keep the hall viable. Also, at that time, Stewart concedes that his location was just a little too far from the beach, even though it was only one mile north of the falls. "People would travel just past the Provincial Park, not see my hall, and figure they had taken a wrong turn and go back," he says.

Stewart's son Steve later took over the building and operated it as an auto body shop. Stewart now owns the popular Kit-Wat Motel on the Sauble River, across from Joseph's Food Store in the north Sauble Beach area.

In 1998 Danceiro is used as a flea market and for winter storage.

Sauble Beach Pavilion

If most people have a favourite dance pavilion that really brings back a memory or stands out in their mind for special reasons, the Sauble Beach Pavilion has to be mine. Not because it was the biggest hall, or because it had the smoothest floor, or because my favourite bands played there - no, Sauble Beach is closest to my heart simply because the pavilion was part of the whole experience of vacationing on this special Lake Huron beach resort area, just a few miles west of Owen Sound.

Although we were far from being considered well-off, our parents always tried to take the family on a vacation for a couple of weeks every summer to escape the city heat. We headed northwest from Weston, to seven miles of the cleanest, purest sandy beach this side of Florida where we could romp through the sand dunes, dive into the waves, buy an ice cream, play the arcades, jump on a trampoline and in later years, dance at the Pavilion.

The Welcome Wagon is always open at Sauble Beach.

My first trip to this little piece of paradise was the summer of 1950, which I can't say I recall in great detail since my needs at the time consisted of a clean diaper, a bottle of milk and plenty of naps. But the few days we spent here apparently convinced my parents and grandparents that Sauble Beach would be a grand place to return each summer. And they did.

It was during this 1950 visit when my parents decided to go dancing at the pavilion one evening. Thanks to some friendly advice from acquaintances they had met, Mom was forewarned to put on a dress for the night. Even though bathing suits and casual clothes were acceptable beach wear during the day, more formal wear was expected of patrons when they attended the dance, even though the wooden pavilion was situated right on the beach. Needless to say, the next generation of young people were allowed entry in much more casual clothing.

It would be another 17 years before I could experience the excitement of entering the pavilion the first time for a dance. Ironically, I was a member of a band that had been hired to play for the evening.

Years before our family discovered Sauble Beach, the original pavilion, called the Octagon after its unique eight-sided shape, was the entertainment centre on the beach. The hall was owned by Bob Walker of nearby Allenford, who had built the hall in 1933, but it was not utilized to a great extent during the Depression years.

In 1945, two couples visited the beach and a chance meeting with Bob Walker would forever change their lives. Wally Scott and his wife, Esther, along with Esther's brother, Jack Robertson and his wife Marg, had taken up an offer from one of Wally's friends to use his cottage at the beach for a week's vacation. Esther picks up the story. "When the two men were out for a walk on the beach one day they met Bob Walker who asked them if they'd be interested in purchasing the pavilion. It also included an old garage and rickety cottage. They said they'd think about it; after a couple of months had passed we returned and Bob asked them again if they wanted the property. A price of $2500 was agreed upon for the business."

Esther says that her husband Wally had two goals: to be self-employed by age 50 and to retire by age 70. They were not unrealistic ambitions and through hard work and shrewd business moves Wally was able to attain both objectives. At the time of purchasing the Octagon, Wally was an accountant with Hepworth Furniture Company in Southampton, a position he held until 1960. Jack Robertson was a public school principal in Cambridge and continued teaching until his retirement.

Wally Scott and his Orchestra.
Top - outside the Pavilion 1946.
Bottom - inside, a few years later.

Wally and Jack were also musicians, both playing trumpet. Wally led his own band, performing regularly at Port Elgin's Cedar Crescent Casino, and it was this orchestra that opened his and Jack's hall July 1, 1946, under its new name, Sauble Beach Pavilion. Wally Scott and His Orchestra became the house band, playing Tuesday, Thursday and Saturday nights; admission was 50 cents.

"The Octagon was rather primitive inside," recalls Esther. "Much of the lumber was still covered in bark, but the men fixed it up. One year later they added a front entrance on the lake side and laid a 40 by 80 foot terrazzo floor to the east so couples could dance under the stars on warm summer evenings. Wally and Jack decided in 1950 that the original structure had to come down, so the old Octagon was flattened, and a new pavilion was built on the same site, leaving the open-air portion as it was."

People who lived in towns in the area came to the Sauble dances, along with beach vacationers, and all were welcomed by Jack who loved to stand at the door and greet his guests with a smile and a handshake. The first night of operation they ran out of change, says Esther.

Jack and Wally were never ones to stand still, and as the beach grew in popularity, attracting vacationers from London, Kitchener/Waterloo, Guelph, Hamilton and even Toronto, the men could see the potential for many new recreational businesses which would cater to this crowd.

"We purchased the bowling alley on the corner of the main street at the lake in 1951," says Esther. "The lanes were completely outdoor, but after we acquired this operation we built a roof over the bowling alleys. They were originally constructed from a masonite material. Not long after this we added a gift store and called the business the Sauble Gift Bowl."

The families' next purchase was a grocery store on the beach between the Pavilion and the Gift Bowl, which they decided to turn into a restaurant. This was the birth of the Driftwood, a restaurant that continues to operate in the 1990's.

Scott-Robertson Enterprises expands to include the Gift Bowl
(which was later enclosed) and the Starlight Roller Rink.

"We seemed to buy every fallen down building in Sauble and then fix it up into some form of business," laughs Esther. Their company also owned a number of cottages and cabins which were used by staff members during the summer. All the businesses created and bought by the company were completely self-financed. "We never borrowed a cent from lending institutions," says Esther. At the time of the acquisitions, both men had their full-time jobs and used their own resources to build the company.

19

Members of both families worked constantly says Esther. "If you walked into the restaurant you picked up a dish cloth and got busy, or took over the cash register. Sundays were really hectic at the Driftwood - sometimes the dishes wouldn't get done until after closing - they were just stored in piles on the floor. Our pancakes were incredibly popular - there was a huge demand for this meal."

Scott-Robertson Enterprises Limited had a staff of 45 - 50 employees, many of whom were students. "They would usually work four hours on and then four hours off. After all, being located on the beach, who could expect kids to work more than four hours without wanting to have some fun!" The Gift Bowl sold immense amounts of beach-related stock and souvenirs during the summers, but the owners were astute buyers and seemed to have a knack to know just which items would be popular the next season.

After operating the Driftwood restaurant for seven years, it was sold and the company bought the Starlight Roller Rink; as with all their businesses, it too was a great success. "We hired a Hanover couple to come and help us three nights per week at the rink - she played the music and he rented the skates," says Esther.

Always on a quest to expand their beach empire, Wally and Jack then purchased the Dahmer Lumber Company on the main corner where the stoplights are located today, and turned it into a restaurant called the Sauble Lights. About the same time they also purchased the remainder of lots in this block.

But even as their empire grew at the beach, the heart and soul of Sauble was the Pavilion. "We always received good crowds at the pavilion," says Esther. The new building with its enlarged interior and outdoor floor could hold up to 2500 dancers - there was no limit put on the numbers because liquor was not sold. Jack and Wally were similar to so many other operators - they gave the crowds good music, warm greetings, and good value for their admission, but in turn they expected no trouble. "If you caused a problem in our hall, you were out forever, that was our policy," says Esther. People also had to dress respectably in the earlier years. Perhaps because of his schoolteaching background, Jack had no trouble receiving respect. He also hired a hefty schoolteacher to work the door.

Being located on the beach so near the water gave the pavilion a very romantic atmosphere for those summer evening strolls. There was usually anywhere from 100 to 400 feet of beach between the lake and pavilion, however, this proximity also gave the men cause for great worry one year in the mid-50's when Lake Huron's level rose to the point where water was actually crashing underneath the pavilion.

"Men from the area sandbagged with Wally and Jack for days," says Esther, "afterwards the entrance was changed to the south side of the building." It also prompted them to purchase township land to the north and east of the pavilion to provide parking for customers. More permanent cribbing and piles of stone were wired together that year for stability and safety of the structure. Some of this work is still visible, though years of wind-blown sand has covered most of it.

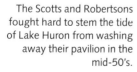

The Scotts and Robertsons fought hard to stem the tide of Lake Huron from washing away their pavilion in the mid-50's.

Along with regular dances, beach people flocked to the Pavilion for weekly bingos, family movies and Wednesday night country dances with Don Robertson's Ranch Boys. The hall was usually kept dark on Sunday nights.

During the Big Band era one of the popular orchestras to play the pavilion on a regular basis was led by Warren Ovens from Kitchener. Warren was not only recognized as a superb trumpet player - he was also one of those few musicians who also had the talent to write great musical arrangements. During Warren's membership in the Swing Patrol in World War II he had the opportunity to perform with some of Canada's best talent.

"In May, 1945, we were the first organized band to play a concert in Amsterdam and we did a command performance for Queen Wilhelmina in that city," Warren told me in late 1994. Back in Canada after the War, Warren's gigs included numerous trips up to Sauble. "We were regulars at the Sauble Beach Pavilion where I knew Wally Scott and Jack Robertson very well. I remember playing many May 24th dances and midnight dances on weekends."

Warren Ovens and his Orchestra from Kitchener were regular performers during the '50's.

KINDLY HANG UP FOR   FUTURE VISITORS' REFERENCE

Vol. 2 No. 6   SAUBLE

HARD WORK...HAPPY

KINDLY HANG UP FOR   FUTURE VISITORS' REFERENCE

SAUBLE BEACH PAVILION

SAUBLE BEACH PAVILION

NEW ENLARGED and RENOVATED

D	TUES.-	FROMAGER BROS. AND THE "SOUNDERS"—
A		Rock 'n Roll — Twist.
N	WED.-	DON ROBERTSON'S FAMOUS RANCH BOYS
C	FRI.-	SEE COLUMN OF FRIDAY SPECIALS
E	SAT.-	BILL WOLFE'S NEW MODERN ORCHESTRA.

CHAMBER OF COMMERCE

THURS.   **B I N G O**   8:15 P.M.
15 Games for 50c.

MOVIES MON. 8:15 P.M.

JULY 2—"CIMARRON"
(Cinemascope)

JULY 9—"PEPE"
(Cinemascope)

JULY 16—"THE ALAMO"
(Cinemascope)

JULY 23—"WACKIEST SHIP IN
THE ARMY"
(Cinemascope)

JULY 30—"THE GUNS OF
NAVARONE"
(Cinemascope)

AUG. 6—"LADIES' MAN"
Laugh with Jerry Lewis

AUG. 13—"AROUND the WORLD
IN 80 DAYS"
(Cinemascope)

AUG. 20—"PILLOW TALK"
(Comedy in Cinemascope)

AUG. 27—"FACTS OF LIFE"
Bob Hope Comedy.

Friday Specials

DANCING PLUS

JULY 6—ANNUAL GIFT NIGHT
Bill Wolfe's Orchestra
Prizes—Passes.

JULY 13—FROMAGER BROS.
and the Country Buddies.

JULY 20—THE CONTINENTALS
A modern Orchestra. Plus
Movie: "Where the Boys Are"

JULY 27—FROMAGER BROS.
Plus Guest—Gordie Tapp

AUG. 3—MISS SAUBLE BEACH
PAGEANT
Bill Wolfe's Orchestra.

AUG. 10—FROMAGER BROS.

AUG. 17—TALENT NIGHT
$50.00 in Prizes.
Bill Wolfe's Orchestra

AUG. 24—FROMAGER BROS.

AUG 31—"MARDI GRAS BALL"
Prizes for Best Costumes.
The Continentals Orchestra

JULY 1972

	TUES.	WED.	THURS.	FRI.	SAT.
	ROCK MUSIC	ADULT DANCE Admission: $1.50	8:15 P.M.	ADMISSION: $1.50 9:15—12:30	ADMISSION: $1.50 9:00 — 12:00
	Admission: $1.50 9:00—12:15	28 TONITE THE DIMENSIONS	EVERY THURSDAY	30 RAIN	1 SEA DOG
	4 NO DANCE TONIGHT	5 DIMENSIONS 9:30 p.m.— 12:45 a.m.	6	7 ATLANTIS	8 IRON ARM
	11 GASLIGHT	12 DIMENSIONS	13	14 HOMESTEAD	15 AMISH
	18 MAJOR HOOPLE	19 DIMENSIONS	20	21 BENTWOOD ROCKER	22 LEIGH ASHFORD
	25 MANCHILD	26 RANCH BOYS	27	28 TIGHTAS	29 GREASEBALL BOOGIE BAND
AUG. 1	TRUCK	2 RANCH BOYS	3	4 YUKON	5 FATHER
	8 NO DANCE MOVIE WOODSTOCK	9 DIMENSIONS	10 SPONSORED BY	11 TO BE ANNOUNCED	12 TO BE ANNOUNCED
	15 TO BE ANNOUNC...	...MBER	17	18 MISS SAUBLE BEACH PAGEANT	19 TO BE ANNOUNCED
	22 MA... HO...				26 TO BE ...ED
	29				

(The letters B, I, N, G, O appear in large print in the Thursday column)

1962

		JULY				
Sun.	Mon.	Tues.	Wed.	Thurs.	Fri.	Sat.
1	2	3	4	5	6	7
8	9	10	11	12	13	14
15	16	17	18	19	20	21
22	23	24	25	26	27	28
29	30	31				

		AUGUST				
Sun.	Mon.	Tues.	Wed.	Thurs.	Fri.	Sat.
			1	2	3	4
5	6	7	8	9	10	11
12	13	14	15	16		
19	20	21	22	2		
26	27	28	29	30		

(Sauble Beach)   1967

SAUBLE BEACH PAVILION

Saturday, May 27th
THE BEDTIME STORY

Wednesday, May 31st
THE SPECTRUMS

Located 140 miles Northwest of Toronto
— On Lake Huron —

Sauble Beach Pavilion

LAKE HURON — ONT.

Saturday, Oct. 11th
THE CHOSEN FEW

Sunday, Oct. 12th
THE COPPER PENNY

The PAVILION Entertainment Centre

MOVIES Mon. - 8:15 p.m.

BINGO Most Tuesdays every Thurs.

DA... SATURDAYS

o Ontario's ROC...

(Sauble Beach)

SAUBLE BEACH PAVILION

LAKE HURON

Fri. . . . The Bedtime Story
Sat. . . . The Magic Circus
"SUNDAY MID-NITE"
LITTLE CAESAR & THE CONSULS

23

Both Wally and Jack were very aware of the changing music tastes of their customers and were not stubborn when it came to accepting the fact that by the 1960's rock `n` roll was on its way and they had better bring it to the Sauble Pavilion if they wished to keep their customers happy. Esther recalls that after they heard the Beatles' music in the early 60's, the men said, "That's it, let's start booking rock!" By the later 1960's, rock dances were held on Tuesday, Friday and Saturday nights, as well as on Sunday midnights during the long weekends. "It was also the time when it became acceptable for girls to dance with girls, since the boys took so long to ask them," adds Esther.

Rock bands were more costly than local orchestras; certain contract demands they made were unreasonable, particularly from some of the well-known groups who would specify items such as the number of meals that had to be provided for them. As the 1970's moved on, some of the bands wanted the audience to sit and watch rather than dance, as the concert aspect of rock became the norm. This riled the operators who believed the purpose of the pavilion was for dancing.

As the price of bands rose, and the drinking age was lowered Jack and Wally decided it was time to think about getting out of the pavilion business. Crowds fell off and the pavilion could not survive on bingo and movies. "The decision to tear the place down was made in the fall of 1978 and that was that!" says Esther. The partners had already started disposing of their other properties in the early 1970's.

Interestingly, no one in the family was sad to see it go down - they were all ready to retire and the workload of maintaining it and the other businesses was tremendous. "My only holiday away from the business was the two week period before Christmas," says Esther. The rest of the year they were travelling to cities and gift shows, purchasing for the Gift Bowl, hiring orchestras, or readying the businesses for the season.

An Owen Sound company was hired to demolish the pavilion. The terrazzo floor was sold off in squares - a minigolf has some, Esther has a couple at her cottage, and a number of other Sauble cottagers likely have a square that felt the dancing feet of hundreds of soles over the years.

The pavilion was the last of the Scott-Robertson Enterprises to go. "We did have a good time during our stay at Sauble," says Esther. "We worked well together, which was fortunate since we were close to one another all the time. There was never a quarrel between the relatives."

The Pavilion was demolished in the fall of 1978 when the partners decided to retire.

Geri Kirkpatrick of Owen Sound has some great memories of the Sauble Beach Pavilion, and here is what she writes:

"Although we lived in Malton, we usually spent most of the summer at the family cottage at Sauble in the still-innocent 1950's. There was a group of about eight of us doing things together. Imagine the reaction of eight young, barely teenage girls when we heard that somehow by coincidence a Canadian Navy ship and an American destroyer had both made port in Owen Sound, and that the crews had liberty. Not one, but two whole ships full of SAILORS! IN UNIFORM! We were beside ourselves with joy. I think the crews probably had some joy as well when they found they had liberty at a beach where there were no doubt a lot of teenage girls.

"I can still see the Latin band at the Pavilion that night with the rows of multi-coloured ruffles on their shirt sleeves, and the stars twinkling perfectly in the sky over the open-air section of the dance floor.

"Our group gravitated towards a similar sized group of American sailors - after all, we could see Canadian boys anytime. One of the boys, Jerry, had been an Arthur Murray instructor in Chicago. I have always been an avid fan of Big Band music and ballroom dancing; we ended up doing almost every dance together, with him teaching me to Rhumba, Mambo and Samba as we went along. Sometimes, we were the only couple on the floor, being cheered for our 'expertise.' During intermission, we had to go out to the edge of the water, so that I could wade in to cool my feet to soothe them from so much dancing.

"I will never forget that wonderful, perfect evening at the Sauble Beach Pavilion. Sometimes when I hear that song COME DANCING, I feel a little sad that the Sauble Beach Pavilion is no longer there, and I relive that great memory of it. This memory still warms my heart."

One of my own favourite recollections of the Sauble Beach Pavilion was the night in 1972 when Canada's great rock group Crowbar performed for a sold-out crowd of well over 2,000. Never did the words "Oh what a feeling, what a rushhhh!!!!!!!" have more meaning.

A modern community centre was built to take up the slack after the pavilion was gone. As Sauble Beach has gradually transformed from a two-month rustic vacation resort into a year-round retirement and winter sports mecca, many events are now held at this facility.

The local history book, *Green Meadows and Golden Sands - A History of Amabel Township* states, "The Pavilion was the focal point of the activities at the Beach for many years, and we doubt if Sauble Beach will ever be the same again as it was when everyone got together and had a whale of a time."

HOLIDAY HOOTENANNY
AT SAUBLE BEACH PAVILION

THE ENTIRE CAST PERFORMS IN THE FINALE.

ENTERTAINMENT NEWS

Dancing Fun

Dancing at the Pavilion is always associated with happiness. No matter what the style of music, its infectious rhythm calls people together, to start moving, to dance, to have fun. People meet people; friendships are made; some fall in love. The lovesongs the bands play become a very personal thing to lovers. The chord changes, the lyrics, the melody all reach the inner soul and the song becomes "our song". The words may change, but the feeling is always deep, true, and enduring.

So another summer at the Pavilion brings exciting groups to provide happy music for you to enjoy, to dance, and to make friends.

Here at Sauble Beach is one of the true summer dance pavilions with its soft romantic atmosphere. Thousands of young people meet here over the season for it is one of those occasions which is a "must" in their summer experience. It is hoped that you will be among them.

WEDNESDAY NIGHT DANCES

Every Wednesday night during July and August (except July 26th and August 2nd) when the good old Ranch Boys will be on the stage, the Pavilion proudly presents the Dimensions, a band that proved so popular last year. This group appeals to a fairly wide age span because its rhythm is based on the modern idiom, and the four-part vocal harmony add a loving touch to the lyrics. The members' appearance and personality on stage has won the acclaim of a wide circle of fans. In short, here is a band with a following.

* Movies

Bingo

Thursday night is another popular family night at the Pavilion for the admission is a low, low 50c. which entitles a player to 15 bingo games. There are three share the wealth specials, and door prizes. A good time is had by all at this Bingo sponsored by the Sauble Beach Chamber of Commerce—8:15 p.m.

The Gift Bowl

Situated at the foot of Main Street, at the water's edge, is an interesting gift and souvenir shop—the Gift Bowl. While browsing around, many summer tourists are pleasantly surprised to find just the right gift from among the hundreds on display for the folks back home or an item for themselves. Here you will find the largest selection of hats, purses and glassware. There's a wide assortment of T-shirts on which you can have your favourite and personal choice of transfer, saying, or motto ironed on.

BOWLING—and here's something new to make your game more pleasurable and exciting—automatic pin setters. At considerable expense, the management has installed this new line of automatic pin setters which you actively control by a series of levers. You'll be fascinated.

Starlight Roller Rink

If you are looking for fun and friends, you cannot go wrong here. This rink is among the best supervised ones in the province and it certainly challenges them all for atmosphere. Year after year, customers meet the same friendly personnel who make them feel at home right away.

At the morning sessions: 10:30 a.m. to 1:00 p.m. (Sundays 1:00 p.m. to 3:30 p.m.), parents are pleased with the care their children receive during the well

Section of the overflow audience who sat, squatted or just reclined on the floor at the Pavilion to enjoy the show put on by "THE LOWDOWNERS", "LONDONTOWNE CRIERS" and "THE GROUP I."

Chapter Four

SOUTHAMPTON - THE BREAKERS LODGE

The site of Southampton's famous Breakers Lodge is just an empty lot overlooking Lake Huron, awaiting development. After 103 years in business, the owners decided to tear down the town's historic hotel in 1991 because, as Marnie Cammidge says, "it was going to cost over $400,000 just to bring it up to current safety standards, and that was too much of an investment for a business operating three months of the year."

Although dancing has not been one of the attractions available to guests in recent years, the Annex at Breakers Lodge was once a popular dance pavilion before it was converted into guest rooms.

William Knowles originally built a large tourist home called Park House, in 1888. He acquired surrounding property, built cottages and created what became known as 'Knowles Park.' His son, Russell, began managing the business in 1918 and built the Dance Pavilion during the 1920's, bringing in well-known orchestras which even included Guy Lombardo. Ferde Mowry's group was also a popular attraction at Lakeview Hotel, as it had been renamed in 1932. Emmett McGrath, who would later purchase Port Elgin's Casino just down the highway, played sax with Ferde at this time. By the late 1930's, Russell's son, William (Biscuit) took over the business, re-named the hotel to the Breakers Hotel and closed the dance hall in favour of creating additional tourist space.

Larry and Elsie Smith bought the Breakers in 1948, with assistance from Frank Newlan who owned the Embassy in Toronto, Ferde Mowry's base. Their daughter, Marnie (Cammidge) began working at the family's hotel, eventually purchasing the business from her parents with her husband in 1969. By now the name had been changed to the Breakers Lodge and consisted of 38 units, a recreational hall and a banquet room. Many original pieces of furniture from 1888 could be found at the Breakers.

Marnie was sad to see such a piece of history disappear. "We had third and fourth generations from families stay with us over the years. I made a lot of good friends. I've also watched many kids grow up, waiting on them when they were babies and then serving their families years later."

Built in 1888 as private home

South's Breakers Lodge

The present day annex was the Dance Hall, where many a famous orchestra played, such as Guy Lombardo and Ferde Mowry. It was made into rooms around 1938. The main lodge has had additions put on, but the original section is still intact. Many of the original pieces of furniture can still be found in it.

Chapter Five

PORT ELGIN - CEDAR CRESCENT CASINO

Of all the dance pavilions along the Lake Huron coastline, Port Elgin's Cedar Crescent Casino was one of the crown jewels. Falling under the jurisdiction of the Stratford Musicians' Association local, owners Emmett and his wife Pat McGrath consider one of the greatest honours bestowed upon them was the recognition by the Union for operating a first-class dance hall.

Being a musician himself, Emmett was particularly pleased at receiving this award. "We were very proud," says Pat, who still resides on one of the resort town's quiet and stately tree-lined streets. "This was a special award based on the facilities, the treatment of the musicians we hired, the quality of sound, size of the crowd, their overall response, and other factors."

An early photo of Cedar Crescent Casino in Port Elgin.

Emmett knew the business from both sides of the stage. As an accomplished sax player, he paid years of dues as a member of the famed Ferde Mowry band who hailed originally from Peterborough, but were probably best known for the 23 years they were the house band at Toronto's Embassy Club on Bloor Street. In fact, it was the Embassy's owner, Frank Newlan, who encouraged the McGraths to make the move into the entertainment business in 1944 when the couple was considering purchasing the Casino. (Emmett and Pat also leased the Arlington Hotel for a few years, a property that Pat's family had owned.)

The Ferde Mowry Orchestra: Top - 1932, Bottom - mid-30's.
Emmett McGrath is standing, far left in the lower photo. Ferde is seated.

Pat and Emmett always took it in good humour when they booked Wally Scott and his orchestra in to the Casino for some of their early spring dances. "Wally and Jack Robertson also owned the Sauble Beach Pavilion, just north of here, so when it was time to open up his own hall a bit later in the season, Wally would start promoting the Sauble Pavilion from our stage," laughs Pat.

Emmett and Pat ran a no-nonsense dance hall, which included everything from monitoring the crowd's behaviour to ensuring the bands were on stage and performed their full contracted number of sets. Says Pat: "When one particular group tried to get away with playing three, 40-minute sets instead of four, Emmett contacted Mr. Carnegie at the Union who told him to take their union cards and refuse to pay them unless they honour their contract - they played four sets!"

It was because of the long (24 years) warm relationship the McGraths had with the people of Port Elgin, the tourists, the bands and the OPP who regularly kept an eye open during dance nights, that Cedar Crescent Casino was regarded with such great affection by everybody connected with the hall. The Port Elgin couple built the Casino into a paradise of wholesome and enjoyable entertainment for all ages. It was not simply a business for them - Emmett and Pat were devoted to the pavilion and pampered it throughout the years, realizing that it was also one of the town's major attractions on the sandy beach.

It was also the reason so many people stood and openly shed tears of grief when the pavilion burned to the ground on Monday, August 17, 1970.

The Casino was 46 years old when it succumbed to the fate of so many of its brothers and sisters. One of the last sections of the pavilion to crumble and fall that sad evening was the main entrance, where every time patrons walked through the doors they could read the words, 'Here's to Life and Laughter - Dance and be Merry Hereafter.'

Built in 1924 by William Brigden and O.E. Boehmer, Cedar Crescent Casino officially opened on June 28th of that year, with a dance featuring The Rainbows of Kincardine. Port Elgin's reeve at the time, Gilbert McLaren, gave the address that evening. The pavilion was operated under the business label of The Port Elgin Amusement Company, with William Brigden as manager. Dances ran six nights per week, attracting hundreds of eager residents and summer vacationers.

Cody and his violin was one of the early entertainers, followed by the Wright Brothers. Emmett even played here for the summers of 1932-1934 with Ferde Mowry's band, and fell in love with the town and the pavilion during these years. Other bands were led by well known musicians of the time, including Ozzie Williams, Brian Farnan and Norm Harris.

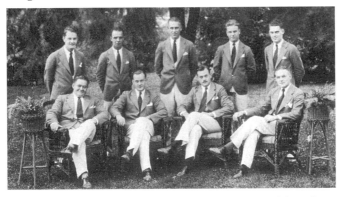

The Wright Brothers, seen in this 1933 photo, were one of the early bands at the pavilion.

Both Ozzie Williams and his Band (above) and Norm Harris with his Orchestra (below) were popular draws wherever they performed throughout Ontario, including Port Elgin.

The 1930's were probably the most festive years at The Casino, with balloons being dropped upon the crowd every Thursday night as the dances ended in a blaze of coloured lights. Dancers popped the balloons and tossed them throughout the pavilion. These were also the days of jitney dances - 15 cents admission and 5 cents a dance - with young lads in blue blazers and white pants roping the dancers on and off the floor throughout the evening.

During the War, dancing was reduced to three nights a week and jitney dancing was replaced with a straight 50 cents admission charge. After William Brigden died, his sister decided to sell the pavilion to Emmett and Pat McGrath in 1945.

Bert Worth and the boys on stage in the mid-40's (above).
The dance floor was always packed at Cedar Crescent Casino (below).

34

From 1950 to 1964 Lloyd Kibbler's Big Band from Owen Sound was the Casino's house band. Lloyd and his orchestra were also regulars at Balmy Beach Pavilion near their home town.

Twelve years after buying the business, Emmett decided to completely renovate the pavilion, revamping the main building and remodelling the bandstand to reflect the changing night-club styles found in many halls. He also added a new extension to the north of the building called The Casino Deck, an open-air dancing area with a terrazzo floor and coloured lights, surrounded with an opaque green glass wall, enhancing the romantic night-time appearance.

As music and dance styles changed, so did the McGrath's music policy. "We had to move with the times," says Pat, even though Emmett's first love was the Big Band music he used to play. The crowds' dress styles were also much different in the 1960's than 20 or 30 years previously.

Bingos were held on Monday nights, Tuesdays were often set aside for a mingling of modern and old-time dancing, and when the Twist became an international craze, Emmett and Pat staged Twist Contests which were run by Port Elgin's Hank Smith, drawing huge numbers of people who came to shake their stuff.

BINGO

Cedar Crescent Casino, Port Elgin

MONDAY

JULY 20

—Ten Free Games for $15.00
—SPECIALS up to $75.00
—SHARE THE WEALTH GAME

Admission: $1.00 — Doors Open At 8:30
Games start at 9 P.M.

Extra or Special Cards: 25c. or 5 for $1

Sponsored by the

PORT ELGIN & DISTRICT CHAMBER OF COM

Emmett McGrath welcomes The Paupers who introduced 'A-Go-Go' - Tues. June 22, 1965.

As the era of rock entered with a tidal wave, bands led by David Clayton Thomas, Ronnie Hawkins, Robbie Lane and many others took over the stage. 'Go-Go' Night was launched by The Paupers in 1965. A regular on Thursday night in the later 1960's was the popular Major Hoople's Boarding House.

For nine summers the Casino rocked to the local sounds of Gordon Rhodes and the Swingin' Comets, featuring the McGrath's sons, Paul and Wayne. Both young men continued in their father's musical footsteps as they grew older. Paul continued performing and teaching music for many years; Wayne today teaches music at Saugeen District High, and plays in the Stardust Big Band.

Emmett and Pat McGrath were proud of their sons Paul and Wayne who played in The Comets. Singer Lynda Lane performed with the group at Port Elgin's Casino.

Wingham's Ranch Boys were popular country and western musicians in Lake Huron's pavilions. As the times changed, so did the music. Emmett and Pat McGrath, like many of their fellow hall owners, moved with the times and started booking rock groups such as The Paupers, Ronnie Hawkins, David Clayton Thomas, Robbie Lane, The Rock Show of the Yeomen, Lords of London and The Copper Penny.

Pat McGrath gives credit to the many people who helped her and Emmett run one of the best halls in the area. "Some of the people who come to mind are Dean Thede, Harry Thede, Bill Kealy, Jack Jacques and Mac Esplen. All of the people on the beach worked hand in hand; we enjoyed those years and made many friends."

Anne Ellis writes with her thoughts: "One of my fondest memories during the War years was the sounds of music wafting over the beach on Saturday nights from the Cedar Crescent Casino. I was too young to attend the dance, but the sight of the coloured lights and the music from the were absolute magic to us kids."

Sheryl Cunningham has a very touching story: "The setting is the Port Elgin Pavilion in July of 1963," she writes. "I was a very shy and lonely 15-year-old with little self esteem. My parents and I were staying at a cottage in Port Elgin for two weeks, but I pretty much kept to myself. I wanted to join in with all the other kids in the area, but just couldn't seem to find the courage to do anything about it.

"When I heard there was a dance taking place at the Pavilion I had no intention of going until I realized that Ronnie Hawkins was performing. I arrived alone and found what I considered the most secluded place to sit. I had barely sat down, when this fellow, extremely intoxicated and 15 years my senior grabbed my arm and said 'You're dancing with me!' Out of nowhere my knight in shining armour appeared and rescued me, calmly and without disturbance. 'There you are, sweetheart, sorry I'm late.' I had never seen this tall, blond-haired, blue-eyed god in my life.

"To keep up the appearance of the charade and avoid further confrontation, he suggested we dance. When I told him I never had and didn't know how, he said 'I'll teach you.' I am an incurable romantic and this evening will always be cherished in my memory. Within four hours I learned how to dance, had my first experience of being held and kissed by a boy, fell in love and was forever changed.

"During the remainder of my stay we were together constantly. When it was time for me to go home, we were heartsick. I returned to high school, he enlisted in the service and was transferred to Nova Scotia for training. We did correspond for two years but saw each other once only briefly. We eventually went in separate directions, meeting and marrying others. I cannot put into the appropriate words the part he played in changing my life. It has always bothered me that I never told him.

"When my first son was born, my husband selected his first name, I chose his second, which just happens to be Allen. This was intended as a tribute to one of the most special people I have encountered in my life - Allen Arthur Masterson. It is unfortunate that he doesn't know it."

In 1968 Emmett and Pat decided to retire from the business and sold the pavilion to James Albrecht and James Buehlow of Walkerton who also owned the Kincardine Pavilion at the time.

Two years later James Albrecht had apparently checked the building about six p.m. in preparation for the evening's bingo game and then left the premises. One hour and 15 minutes later the pavilion was ablaze. Two hours later there was nothing but scorched timbers and black smoking debris remaining on the beach.

One week after the devastating fire that completely destroyed one of Port Elgin's most famous landmarks and main tourist attractions on the beach, Mrs. Helen Hammond submitted the tribute she composed about her favourite pavilion, which was printed in the Port Elgin Times Newspaper. This wonderful piece of prose expresses the history, the significance and the heartfelt loss that represents the feelings of so many people when they think about Port Elgin's famous pavilion:

To A Dance Hall

"Poor old Casino!"
"Dear old Friend!"

Numbly we watch, with unbelieving eyes -
The fierce, hot flame, so swift, so cruel -
The last remaining timbers, charred and bent -
The smoking ruin of your grave -
Then, mercifully, darkness covers you.

Dumbly we watch, but through our sadness
Memories and the sound of music come
Crowding and dancing on the summer air.

Jazz music from the Twenties,
When you were young and gay -
Don Wright and College slickers,
Charming your first dancing feet.

White-flannelled, blazered beaus, proud of
Flappers with close-bobbed hair,
Dancing apart the Charleston Rag -
"Yessir, She's my Baby!" - "Ain't She Sweet?"

Embassy's Ferde Mowry with the big band sound -
City glamour for a lakeside town -
Tuxedoed, handsome men, with musical perfection -
And one returned to join his life with you.

Girls in gaily-coloured summer frocks -
Boys, white-jacketed, clean and smooth,
Swaying, swinging to the "Star-dust" tunes.
And bright-eyed kids who thought themselves as lucky,
Roping the floor and taking jitney tickets
From eager couples paying "Ten Cents a Dance."

After the reign of Jimmy Barber,
"Pied Piper with a saxophone" -
Lean, empty years, when strong men
Were gone to win a bloody war.

Years, tunes, gay figures flitting by, too quick to catch,
The end of big band swinging sound -
Small groups, electrified to power -
A blaze of "Comets," young and gay,
Who, in their bright flame of life
Warmed all who danced and listened.

To the now-young, colourful and free -
Blue-denimed, long-haired look-alikes,
Dancing apart to the wild, wild beat
Of "Mythical Meadow," "Copper Penny" groups,
Amplified to rock and blow the mind -
Or soothe it sweet with "Raindrops," cool,
And "Midnight Cowboy" - lovely tunes.

Then sudden silence - sight and sound are stilled,
Burned from our grieving beach, bereft and bare.

There's some who think that this is as should be -
"Good-bye and good riddance!" is their cry,
But they should not be quick to throw the stone
By judging by their own misspent young hours.
While in our yesterdays you still live on,
Dreams cannot serve young dancing feet.
We voice a hope, a plea, to those
Who hold the doubtful future in their hands
That on you cold, dead ashes may soon rise
A new Casino, named the same.

That it be gracious, as you were gracious,
With wide, low, sheltered steps, inviting all.
That it be lovely, as you were lovely,
With shuttered promenade, opening to the cool, night air.
That it be charming, as you were charming,
With softly glowing lights and jewel-bright stand.
That it have music, worthy of the time,
Both for the young and for the young in heart -
That it have welcome room for all
To meet, to dance, to play - perchance, to dream.

On Monday August 17 1970, Port Elgin's Cedar Crescent Casino was destroyed by fire.

In a short piece he wrote for the same newspaper, Kevin Rigg expressed his sadness at the loss of the Casino. He writes: "To drive on the Port Elgin beach … in years before … you could remember the warm nights full of sound and happiness and young people dancing. Now the one thing which held so many memories is gone! When the Casino died, so died part of the community, the free spirit of youth died. The only hopes which can be seen in the ashes are those of having a new building constructed."

Both Helen Hammond's and Kevin Rigg's dreams were realized soon after the Casino burned. A new pavilion was constructed and continued to run dances and other community events for about ten years. Unfortunately, this brand new hall was condemned as being structurally unsafe on the sandy beach and was demolished, a scant few years after opening; some say that when the demolition process began, it was obvious the building was not in as delicate

Here we see the Port Elgin landmark, the Cedar Crescent Casino before later renovations. The building burned down in August of 1970.

The Port Elgin Casino: *'Let's face the music and dance'*

by Tim Cumming
Shoreline News

during the seasons of 1932, 1933 and 1934.)

Port Elgin's Hank Smith. Music changed over the —d Rock

PORT ELGIN

"THE TOWN OF MAPLES"

83rd Year   No. 33   Wednesday, August 19, 1970

Page 20 — THE PORT ELGIN TIMES, Wednesday, August 26, 1970

To A Dance Hall

Written and contributed by (Mrs.) Helen Hammond

PORT ELGIN CASINO DEMOLIS'

by
Florence Stafford

Shortly before seven-fifteen on Monday evening, fire broke out in the Cedar Crescent Casino on Port Elgin Beach.

Despite heroic efforts by the Fire Department, the flames appeared throughout the building, and it was completely razed in less than two hours.

Built in 1924 by Bill Brigden, the Casino was operated by the late E. O. Boemer until 1944 when it was purchased by Mr. E. McGrath, of Port Elgin, who, in turn ran it for 24 years.

Two years ago Mr. McGrath sold the building to Mr. James Albrecht and Mr. James Buehlow both of Walkerton. They are also co-owners of the Dance Pavilion in Gacardine.

In an interview with Jim Albrecht, he told this reporter that fire had been in the building around 6 p.m., at which time he was checking the grill and fryer to make sure they were not on, and had then gone up to Southampton for an hour or so before coming back to prepare for the bingo which was to be held on Friday evening.

He went on to say that at the present, his main concern is getting the debris off the beach, which is the responsibility of the owners, but that although it has been a devastating experience, they would like to rebuild, as they have been on the property for another eight years.

Both Jim Albrecht and Jim Buehlow were high in their praise of the Fire Department, and all who helped.

PORT ELGIN CASINO

Nostalgia Is All That's Left

They came, hundreds strong, that day last week to watch the savage destruction of wh ' has been Port Elgin's oldest and proudest recre   ndmark.

For some, it was a spectacle   nding a suppertime theatre of thrills   Only enjoyment of unrehearsed ev those who really knew the able history of the "Casi" to the mundane history

Before these eyes, f every timbered joint bustible material of tentacles of fire, v their path, until ed as sorrowful and sounds of gaiety for th

The Po ter, was And no the sal It sur had fir

GHOST HAUNTS PORT ELGIN
by Kevin Rice

To drive on the pier for Port Elgin beach leaves one with a cold feeling of desolation. An empty beach with the wind and the white beach with the never been there before. The water is barren, the sand dunes are departing the beach.

Crescent Casino came into being. Serenaded by "The Rainbows" of Kincardine, it's formal opening, with a large crowd in attendance, saw Port Elgin's then Reeve, the late Gilbert McLaren, make the official address.

Although named the Cedar Crescent Casino, the enter prise bore the business title of The Port Elgin Amuse ment Company, with William Brigden as manager. Open

"c dancing was here to stay. The promise was ..I, for it soon became the habit of hundred Elgin nightly, except Sunday, to enjoy the only truly dance pavilion on Lake

e years ticked on, The Casino became d more a magnet for residents and holiday ce routines became evident, greater "name were summoned for the June, July and ..sons.

and his violin was one of the originals, followes first really organized dance band in the persons of famous Wright Brothers. The noted Canadian .e band of Ferde Mowry, of Toronto, played during : seasons of 1932—33—34. It was with this band that .ast owner of the Casino, Emmett McGrath, who 's Sax at Toronto's famous Embassy, embarked ~t venture in Port Elgin.

. the Casino operated six nights a night was always a special occasion. .g, strung from the ceiling were filled ., some containing prizes. Near the closing might, the flags were dumped of their con .undreds of balloons fell to the outstretched he dancers to pop and float at will, creating Gras effect while rays of colored lights played m, to add to the gaiety of the scene.

Jitney dancing" was then the vogue. Admission . 15 cents per person; dances were 5 cents each. .ys in blue coats and white pants, stationed at the .oxes which served the purpose of "receipt and custom greeted patrons as they stepped on to the floor. But the "jitney" price was short-lived. With the war came a change. The Brigdens were forced to curtail activi ties to three nights a week and the "jitney price" gave way to a straight 50 cents admission charge.

With the passing of Mr. Brigden the Casino entered a new era. His sister, the late Miss Kate Brigden, always

The re-modelling of the Casino, while under their care, brought the building up to standards acclaimed by all patrons as second to none of any pavilion of its kind. The McGraths were landlords for 24 years, long er than even the original founders.

It was 46 years ago that the late William Brigden and O. E. Boehmer built the Casino. That was in 1924. It was on the night of June 28th, of that year that Cedar

44

shape as originally thought and likely could have been repaired. In any case, the site where both pavilions once sat is now a vast beach where every summer thousands of people now sunbathe, play volleyball and sail, most of them oblivious to the decades of dancing that took place on the very spot where their over-sized beach towels are spread.

On the bright side, Big Band music continues to live even though the Casino is just a memory; enthusiasts now gather every September in Port Elgin to attend the annual Big Band Celebration which began in 1995. This festival continues to grow, attracting both musicians and music fans from all over the province. Pat McGrath figures prominently as one of the town's organizers for this popular musical salute.

To close the chapter on Port Elgin, let's read the words of Emmett McGrath from a 'Jayceegram' written in 1957: "And as the brilliant summer sun sinks slowly in all its colourful splendour into beautiful Lake Huron, the romantic overtures of Kibbler's music drifts into the night, mingled with laughter and the downbeat of the jitterbug to the slow dreamy-eyed movements of young lovers, gliding to and fro completely engrossed in the enchantment of the night. With this we silently steal away contented that today, here in Port Elgin, we have the Cedar Crescent Casino. An amusement centre for young and old that offers completely relaxing fun to thousands and a magnetic influence to our summer industry."

The re-modelled pavilion (below left).   Big Band music continues to thrive in Port Elgin.

45

Chapter Six

INVERHURON PAVILION

Long before the Bruce Nuclear Generating Station was even a glow in Ontario Hydro's eyes, the small community of Inverhuron, just south of the site, had its own power plant in full operation during the summer months, as dancers created their own unique energy at the Inverhuron Dance Pavilion.

The last dance was held here over 30 years ago, but the building - now converted into apartments - sits on a large lot, and is a reminder of the exciting times that took place underneath the metal roof. On a windy day, Lake Huron's waves can be heard as they break and roll into shore, a couple of blocks to the west.

The Inverhuron Pavilion was converted into apartments in the mid-1960's.

George Scott was the last person to run dances at the pavilion and still owns the building today. I spoke with George in late 1994 in the home he built on the rear portion of the hall's lot and where he lives with his wife. Now in his late 70's, George served with the Royal Canadian Navy in WWII as engineer on two Bangor class minesweepers - the Drummondville and the Medicine Hat.

George was born in Stratford and became involved with music at an early age. His instrument was violin, which he played in a string quartet; he then progressed to bass in dance orchestras.

"Before the War, starting at about 16 or 17 years of age, I played with Tony Cryan and His Band in all the towns within a radius of about 45 miles of Stratford; I also attended dances as a customer," says George. "All the fellows had regular day jobs, so we couldn't travel too far." The group played towns and cities like Woodstock, London, Kitchener, Puslinch Lake, Mitchell and Seaforth. The group had a running repertoire of over 150 songs, and travelled to their gigs by Cadillac, trailer and a Fargo one-ton panel truck, always polished and painted with the silhouette of a couple dancing and the logo 'Music Styled For You - Tony Cryan and His Band.' George's orchestra had a reunion back in 1993. "Some of the boys hadn't seen one another since before the War."

George Scott (far right in photo) was a member of the Tony Cryan Band, based in Stratford.

Remembering the Big Band era
Story of Tony Cryan and his Band to be preserved at museum

"I always liked playing dance halls, and hoped for years for the chance to run my own pavilion. When I saw the ad for this hall in a London newspaper I took the plunge," says George.

The Inverhuron hall was built in 1930 by Mr. McCarthy, changing hands to people such as Mr. Mahood and other owners, until Mr. Collins took it over and sold to George in 1948. George says that it was impossible to get insurance on dance halls, "because they did have a reputation for going out of business, and of course the wooden structures were a fire risk." Therefore, he carried no insurance.

The hall was very busy, catering mostly to the many farmers who would come out faithfully from the Kincardine and Port Elgin countryside. "The farmers were very careful with their money - I'd watch them pull out their wallets from their pockets and very slowly unzip them as they paid their admission."

Local bands were usually hired, playing music for both round and square dancing. "We had three squares per night - Skipper McKinnon was one of the best callers. The kids always followed him home after the dance, to make sure he got back safely." At its peak, Inverhuron's crowds were often 400-plus. "I had a snack bar as well, which was another busy part of the hall."

George ran dances until the mid-1960's when he could see the impact that other entertainment forms such as television and bars were having on his dance business. "With the new TV stations opening in Wingham and Kitchener, television was much more accessible to people in the area and this affected my attendance. The crowds began to dwindle, so I closed the hall in 1964." George was very sad when he made the decision to shut down the pavilion, but as he says, it would have been hard to sell an empty building that did not really have a purpose any longer. However, since his pavilion was on his own private land, George was free to do what he wanted with the building. "I renovated the hall and converted it into apartments, originally for summer residents, but a few years later I winterized them for year-round tenants."

George enjoyed his 18 years in the business. His philosophy was to give everyone a fair deal. "I was able to get the bands at a reasonable rate, and this was reflected in the fair admission price I charged - I wanted to keep all costs down for the folks."

The music is no more at Inverhuron - the only humming you'll hear today is the electricity surging through the Bruce's transformers.

Chapter Seven

KINCARDINE PAVILION

The building rests so close to Lake Huron that large boulders and tons of fill are its only protection from the angry spume Lake Huron can produce. For 75 years The Kincardine Pavilion has sat on the town's beach; it has survived July's blistering heat and January's northwest gales, and continues to this day to be a year-round gathering spot for people.

The Kincardine Pavilion is the only hall of its kind still operating along this stretch of Lake Huron.

For many years during the summer months hundreds of local residents and vacationers from out of town subscribed to the Bluewater Summer Playhouse professional theatre productions which were presented in the pavilion. Today, this building with 'the finest dance floor this side of Sarnia' hosts many functions such as wedding receptions, private dances, meetings and reunions.

The pavilion has been renovated and generally spruced up quite extensively in recent years. The original entrance at the north end was long ago closed, and manicured gardens and decorative planters now welcome guests as they enter through the addition which was added to the east.

The Kincardine Pavilion is the last operating original dance hall on Lake Huron.

The interior walls have received a fresh coat of dark blue paint in keeping with the original colour, and the lustrous dance floor has been carefully refinished. This floor is actually comprised of three layers of wood, topped off with hardwood strips. To enhance the rustic atmosphere of the building, the ceiling is clad in tongue-and-groove strips of pine. A balcony from the second level overlooks the large dance floor; originally, bands were to play up in this balcony, but as the orchestras became larger in size there was simply not enough room for them. A stage was then constructed at the south end of the building.

It was George Conley back in 1922 who felt that it was time for the town to have a dedicated dance hall. Previously, dances were held in the old agricultural building at Connaught Park. This energetic individual designed and even helped to fund the new pavilion and in 1923 it was officially opened during the Old Boys and Girls Reunion which was held July 16th to the 23rd.

The land on which the building sits was acquired by the town of Kincardine in 1884, when it purchased lots from Levi Rightmeyer. Pavilion owners have all leased this land from the town.

Although George Conley held the mortgage on the hall, the first actual owners and operators were Reuben Wittig and Tony Campbell. From the earliest dances, the floor was maintained fastidiously. Equal parts of cornmeal and wax were applied by shaving blocks of paraffin, which was worked into the floor by the swaying couples. The cornmeal also helped to keep the floor smooth.

Dances used to run four nights per week during the summer months. As with all of the beach pavilions, couples would saunter along the beach during the evening, while others just sat and enjoyed the music floating through the open shutters and into the evening air. On the rare occasion that an event was scheduled in the winter, large wood and coal stoves were fired up at least two days before the dance in order to warm up the pavilion.

Inside the hall was a large circular light that looked like a moon when illuminated. It was customary to turn on this light whenever a song was performed with the word 'moon' in the title, and also for the last dance of the night. Paper dresses were available for rent if a young woman was wearing shorts at the beach during the day and wished to attend the dance at night.

A number of owners have taken turns operating the Kincardine Pavilion. Reuben and Tony continued their partnership until 1941 when Reuben moved out of town - he still retained his interest in the business, however. Tony Campbell and his wife then held the reins until 1947. At this time Reuben sold his share to Clarence Mullen who took over the full business in the 1950's with his wife Hazel. In 1970 the couple sold to James Buehlow and James Albrecht; these partners ran a number of events in the hall including banquets and various amusements. The pavilion then sat vacant for a couple of years until the Kincardine Kinsmen purchased the building in 1981 and began a project of improving the structure. For over 12 years the pavilion has been owned by Jeff Palmateer and Bill Graham.

From the lake side, large boulders protect the pavilion from Huron's brutal force.

Music of every type from Big Band, to country, to rock 'n' roll has been performed at the Kincardine Pavilion. One of the early local bands to play was Giles Merrymakers. Other orchestras who travelled to this resort community included Don Messer, Lionel Thornton, Mart Kenney and the John Brenan band.

Jim Steele played sax with the Brenan band many years ago and remembers the Kincardine Pavilion with great affection. He says, "Our group was so well known that we developed quite a following of regular fans who would show up each week. Some of them were from London who owned cottages in the area. They all had their regular tables in the hall and responded enthusiastically, giving the band great support." Since then, Jim and his family have cottaged near Kincardine for many years.

Another popular London band to perform at Kincardine was Johnny Downs and his Orchestra. In the summer of 1939 they persuaded Tony Campbell to book their newly formed band. Johnny remembers Tony as "a likeable old Scot never without his trademark cigar stub in his mouth - and he made us work!" During those summer months the eight members were able to become "something cohesive enough to be called a dance band," as Johnny puts it. "We were non-union at that time, but Tony made us sign a contract that bound the band to rehearse every morning at ten a.m., start playing every night at nine and continue playing until Tony said the dance was finished." Johnny says that the floor at Kincardine was as smooth as a bowling alley.

Orangemen's Day was the biggest event of the year in Kincardine at that time; the band was instructed to start playing at noon, and keep playing until five. "Then we had two hours off and started again at seven, for the rest of the night," says Johnny, who played sax. "At the end of that day my teeth had gone through my bottom lip."

That summer each member of the band was paid twelve dollars per week, with Johnny as leader making an extra four bucks. "The band received commission on amounts over one hundred dollars at the door," explains Johnny. "On Orangemen's Day we made more money on that one day than we did all week." Accommodations were nearby in an old cottage that the band rented for a hundred dollars for the season.

Johnny Downs led one of London's top bands, playing his unique brand of "Sophisticated Swing," as seen in this 1953 photograph. In his early career, Johnny and his band mates paid their dues in pavilions such as Kincardine's.

V. MisKimins used to dance at this pavilion and writes, "I feel the young people of today are missing out on the romance of dancing under the stars and the fun and friendliness of pavilions. I have happy memories of the Kincardine Pavilion on the shores of Lake Huron where Mart Kenney and several other big bands played. During intermission how nice it was to take a stroll along the lakefront."

Kincardine resident and businessman Mike Palmer is with the well-known Lighthouse Swing Band which has performed in the area since its inception in 1984. Mike played regularly in both the Kincardine Pavilion and numerous other venues early in his musical career, and today his band, featuring Shelley Parker on vocals, continues to appear at annual Big Band concerts in nearby Port Elgin and Thornbury.

Another resident of the town, Charles Merritt says that the hall is often referred to as the 'Beach Pavilion'; he also remembers the many bands which "have come north to play for an evening dance."

With Ontario Hydro having been the largest employer in the area for many years, Kincardine has attracted many new residents who have grown to love this picturesque and historic town on Lake Huron. Visitors who take the Heritage Walking Tour around Kincardine have 44 sites to view. The Pavilion is Number 15. Don't miss it.

BIG BAND

The Lighthouse Swing Band

*F*ormed a little over four years ago, the Lighthouse Swing Band specializes in the dance music of the 1930's and 40's. The group is made up of seventeen area musicians and a female vocalist. Many members of this group are veteran musicians who have played in big bands for decades and simply love to recreate the sounds of a by-gone era. Original arrangements used by orchestras such as Glenn Miller, Duke Ellington and Harry James have helped the band capture a sound that is rarely heard today.

For further information contact: Mike Palmer, (519) 396-7521, Kincardine.

Chapter Eight

GODERICH - PAVILION/HARBOURLITE INN

The headlines in the first 1947 issue of the 'Goderich Pavilion Dance News' whetted dance fans' appetites for the upcoming season. After a long cold winter, 'The Pav' was ready to open its doors once again, featuring bands like Ted Pudney, Bobby Gimby, Johnny Downs, Stan Patton, Mart Kenney and Art Hallman.

The lead article reads: "Overlooking the blue water of Lake Huron at Goderich, The Goderich Pavilion has long been the favourite dance spot with residents and visitors to 'The Prettiest Town in Canada.'"

Admission prices that year: 75 cents per person on Saturday nights, 50 cents on Wednesday nights.

The Pav.

As with Goderich's dance hall, many of the pavilions around Ontario had other names, but these halls were known to regulars simply as 'The Pav.' When you told somebody "See you at The Pav," they knew where you'd be. Even when owners Leah and Roy Breckenridge re-named the hall to the Harbourlite Inn, people still referred to it as The Pav.

MEET ME AT THE
PAVILION
GODERICH
Friday, May 24
Dance to Music by
Bill Robinson
and his 9-piece orchestra
of London.
Dancing every Saturday
Night Thereafter

Before the Breckenridges took over the reins, the pavilion had been owned by the Buchanan family. In 1920 James Buchanan put forth his plans for building the hall, and within six months it had been constructed by the Goderich Amusement Company Ltd. for a cost of $12,000. Over one thousand people attended the official opening in June, 1920, with the London Orchestra providing the music. The 36 by 90 foot dance floor could comfortably hold 225 couples who danced jitney style in the early days.

Born in Goderich, Roy was a musician himself and ran a music store in town for many years. He began managing the local dance pavilion in 1940 for a friend who owned the business. While Roy was in the army during the War years, his wife Leah took over management duties. In 1947 Roy was given the opportunity to purchase the hall and decided to go ahead with the plan. The stage was immediately enlarged to accommodate the big bands that performed here and it was at this time that Roy also started publishing his newsletter, 'Dance News' to keep people informed of upcoming dances and entertainers.

"Everyone went to The Pav," Leah told me in late 1995. It was the place to meet your friends and have a great time. And best of all, soon after Roy and Leah took over, they winterized the pavilion so it could operate year-round. When the Breckenridges were approached by Barb Cutt in the early 1950's to cater her wedding in the hall, the door was opened to a whole new world of possibilities. "But first, we had to equip the hall with everything you require to cater to large groups, and that included tables, chairs, china, cutlery and so on," says Leah. However, once the material was in place, the pavilion became the choice of many people for dinners and receptions.

"That's why the name was changed from the Goderich Pavilion to the Harbourlite Inn; we felt the name gave the hall more of a classier image for wedding receptions and other functions," says Leah. A 'Name The Pav' contest was held to change the name, with two individuals winning prizes - Ebb Ross and Mrs. Eugene MacAdam. But it was still called The Pav by regulars.

"Name The Pav" contest winners (below left); first catered wedding at The Pav (right).

The couple became members of the Association of Dance Hall Operators, and got to know people such as Gerry Dunn, Don Ivey and Harry Law who were on the Board of Directors. It was London dance hall entrepreneur Harry Law who suggested a special form of wax that they should use on the dance floor.

Many Goderich residents can still recall working part-time at the pav for various functions. "We hired a lot of young people when we catered various events over the years," says Leah.

One of those people was Robert McKee who writes, "For several years I worked part-time at the Harbourlite Inn, starting out in the coat check room, sweeping floors, taking tickets, painting, cutting grass, etc. When I finally turned 21, tending bar was a great step up. It was a fine old wooden building with a hardwood floor (powder waxed). A large curved bar was off to one side in a wing off the dance floor, and there were full kitchen facilities behind the bar for catering banquets and wedding receptions."

New Year's Eve, 1947. Sitting are Joe Allaire and his wife, Dorothy.

(It should be noted that liquor was restricted to private functions using special occasion permits; Roy had applied for, and been issued a permit to serve alcohol for the public dances, but decided not to use it, feeling that the additional restrictions a licence would put on his establishment might affect the original atmosphere of the pavilion.)

Both Roy and Leah formed long-term friendships with many of the entertainers who played at the Harbourlite Inn. Leah considers Johnny and Dorothy Downs from London and Paul Cross from Stratford to be among her best friends. London area bands were extremely popular at The Pav, and included ones such as Lionel Thornton and the Casa Royal

The Pav, under its new name, just before it was torn down in the 1970's

Memories of The Pav: dance hall days

BY SONIA BJORKQUIST

The era of big band music ... long passed, but the memories of ... hall days ... still hold stro... people...

For more than 50 ... Pavilion stood on Ea... lever of the roaring ... big bands in the ... spunk of cour... 1950's, and th... in the 1960... The Pa... Pav, ... hear... y...

the Pav officially opened ... with a crowd of over a thousand atten-ding, according to an article in The Signal of June 27. The six-piece London Orchestra was the first to play in The ...

... an eve... celebrate holida... "Everybody w... all dressed up on ... Roy's wife Leah.

Goderich Pavilion

DANCE NEWS

LAKE
HURON'S
SMARTEST
DANCE
SPOT!

GODERICH, ONTARIO   July, 1947

Outstanding Bands Coming!

God...
demoli...
He rec...
during its e...
bought the dan... an...
family. James Buci...
the town establish a...
in January 1920, an...
building (costing $1 1...
within six months...
Amusement Compar...

Hallowe'en Dance
GODERICH PAVILION
FRIDAY, OCTOBER 29
PAUL CROSS ORCHESTRA ADMISSION 75...
DANCING 9 to 1 ... SPONSORED BY BETA SIGMA PHI

Advance Sale
of Tickets for

ART HALLMAN
HERE JULY 12th

hit everywhere as leader of Canada's
ce-band sensation, Art Hallman and his
come to the Goderich Pavilion on
July 12th.

a might well be proud of Art Hallman
I town boy who rose from a choir boy
ler of his own dance-band! Born in
Ontario, Art and his family took up
in Vancouver B.C., when he was less
ear old. ... musical debut
the Su...
concert

LAKE
HURON'S
SMARTEST
DANCE
SPOT!
Goderich Pavilion
DANCE NEWS
GODERICH, ONTARIO   August, 1947

RETURN ENGAGEMEN

BOBBY GIMBY

More Big Bands Coming!

CIVIC HOLIDAY SPECIALS

ALF TIBBS' 15-PIECE BAND
Comes to "PAV" Civic Holiday

Saturday Aug. 2

The Skyliners
WITH VOCALISTS
JULIA DUNSEITH
and
CLAYTON BRODHA...
Admission The pe...

Sunday, ...
Au...

Scott...

MU...
Admission 50c ...

AUGUST PARADE OF BANDS

such ...
lly wo ... JULIA DUNSEITH
ognize... and CLAYTON BRODHAGEN
music.
ocali... SUNDAY, MID-NIGHT
is be SCOTTY McLACHLAN
he's And His Music for Moderns
hit MONDAY, AUG ...
tucs ALF TIBBS
t... AND HIS GREAT BAND
ie, SCOTTY McLACHLAN
... SATURDAY, AUG ...
l u... WED...
st ... THE L...
d Halli...

SATURDAY, AUG 2nd
THE SKYLINERS

SATURDAY, AUG 16th
WEDNESDAY, AUG 20th
SCOTTY McLACHLAN

WEDNESDAY, AUG 23rd
BOBBY GIMBY
AND HIS BAND
Featured Trumpeter with the
Happy Gang

WEDNESDAY, AUG 27th
SCOTTY McLACHLAN

SATURDAY, AUG 30th
THE SK...

**ADVANCE
TICKET SALE**
Bobby Gimby
THE PAV.
Saturday, Aug. 23
The Music Sho...
A...

who has a

GODERICH PAVILION
LABOR DAY WEEK-END DANCING
THE LAST FRIDAY NIGHT TEEN AGE DANCING
WITH JOHNNY WALTERS OF CFPL, CANADA'S YOUNGEST
DISC JOCKEY AT M.C.
SATURDAY AND SUNDAY, MIDNIGHT—BILL STUART
AND HIS ORCHESTRA
EVERY WEDNESDAY NIGHT IS SQUARE DANCE NIGHT.

GODERICH PAVILION
DANCING WEDNESDAY AND SATURDAY NIGHTS
SATURDAY NIGHT—MUSIC BY JOHNNY BRENAN AND
HIS ORCHESTRA.
EVERY WEDNESDAY NIGHT IS SQUARE DANCE NIGHT
with CLARENCE PETRIE and the NIGHT HAWKS.
Special Mid-night Dance May 23rd, at 12.05 to 3 a.m. Paul
Cross and his orchestra.
Special May 24th Holiday Square Dance 70 to 1 a.m. Clarence
Petrie's Nighthawks.

GODERICH PAVILION

For one night
Louis Armst...
Every W...
Johnny D...
and his

ANNIVERSARY D...
Night—Tear...
Square Dance by Jerr...

June 25...

LAKE
HURON'S
SMARTEST
DANCE
SPOT!

60

Orchestra, Neil McKay and his orchestra, Scott McLachlan, Ted Pudney and bands led by Johnny and Bobby Downs. Often a band would be booked for the season in the early years of operation, such as Neil McKay's group. "They were just young fellows at the time," says Leah. "They stayed at a nearby cottage for the summer and we acted as chaperons. A few of the members even sang in church every Sunday. When they weren't playing at our place, Roy would book them into other halls in nearby towns like Kincardine and Bayfield, so they could keep working."

Neil McKay, who brought his orchestra to The Pav in Goderich during his high school years, was the only member of his band to make music his career, although the others are doctors, business executives and teachers.

Neil McKay was one of the most gifted musicians to play Goderich and became a favourite of Roy and Leah. His orchestra included Jack Walters, drums; Bob Livingstone, bass; Ted Walker, trombone; Don Galpin & Jack Disher, trumpets; Roy Allison, piano; Jack Byes, Don Struthers, Eric Vogen and Neil McKay, saxophones.

"Neil McKay formed his first dance band at the age of 16," writes Dr. Morris P. Wearing, a retired London obstetrician whose passion has always been Big Bands, particularly local talent. "He was forced to write his own arrangements because he could not afford to buy 'stocks.' During the winter of 1940-41 they played at Warner Hall for service men's dances. In the fall of 1943 Neil and his orchestra became the house band at the London Arena."

Neil McKay is now Dr. McKay. The thousands of people who danced to his band's music in pavilions all over western Ontario might never have guessed that years later this musician would have received his Doctorate in musical composition, travelled 8,000 miles in Africa to record primitive music, and taught music at Wisconsin State University and in Hawaii.

At a reunion held a few years ago, the band members reminisced about some of the gigs they played back in the 1940's. One of the fondest recollections was the summer of 1942 at Goderich, where the band stayed in an old house for the season while performing at the pavilion. They also recalled the summer of 1941 when they made the grand salary of $15 per week each at the pavilion in Kincardine. Between 1938 and 1944 the band played hundreds of gigs around London.

The men still enjoy the music they played in their youth, and some of them even get together for the occasional jam session. The names of the members of Dr. McKay's orchestra are: Dr. Jack Byles (sax), Dr. Eric Vogen (sax), Dr. Jack Walters (drums), George Hartsell (piano), Don Galpin (trumpet), Don Stothers (sax), Ted Walker (trombone), Jack Disher (trumpet), Bob Livingston (bass) and Roy Allison (piano).

Neil McKay's band is an example of the great talent that came out of London during the Big Band era. In Dr. Wearing's opinion, "Neil was the best academic dance band musician to come from London. His music was always a bit different; his arrangements had imagination."

Bobby Downs and his Orchestra were regulars at Goderich.

Jack Evans, Art Hallman and Bert Niosi were respected Canadian musicians and orchestra leaders who put Goderich on their gig itinerary.

Lionel Thornton and his Casa Royale Orchestra from London were crowd pleasers.

Stratford sent the Skyliners, another great dance band.

Scotty McLachlan led a popular orchestra.

As time moved along, Wednesday night at The Pav was devoted to country and western music. "Frankly, Roy and I were not country music fans, but we realized that many people did like this music, and in fact some of our best crowds turned out for the Wednesday dances." Teen dances were big as well, with recorded music provided by a disc jockey from CKNX (the local radio station in Wingham broadcasting to western Ontario). "Those nights were very popular," says Leah. The Breckenridges advertised extensively on radio, newspaper and plastered posters around the area.

When the town fathers were finally convinced that midnight dances would not corrupt the population, Roy and Leah were given permission to stage these traditional long-weekend affairs. Interestingly, the Harbourlite Inn's property taxes were higher than those of the local hotel.

Roy tried to keep the hall as busy as possible, with dances two nights per week, bingos, service club dinners and dances, and other private receptions.

The couple finally decided in 1972 that it was time to retire from the business they had operated for 30 years. "The land was really the valuable portion of the property - it was worth more than the building," says Leah. New Year's Eve, 1972, was an emotional time for the 500-plus who turned out to say goodbye to The Pav - the Goderich dance pavilion which had been so much a part of their lives. In 1973 the land was sold and the contents of the hall were auctioned, including the dance floor. The building was then demolished.

The Essex Street location on which the Harbourlite Inn sat shares no visible clue to the good times that people once had at their Goderich pavilion. Residential housing now hides all traces of The Pav, where people once danced high above the shore of Lake Huron.

Chapter Nine

BAYFIELD PAVILION - JOWETT'S GROVE

The couple on the microfilm machine beside me in the Goderich library smiled and exchanged a brief mischievous grin. "Oh yes," they laughed, "we certainly remember the Bayfield Pavilion, especially during the 60's and 70's when we attended dances. Those were good times - maybe a fight outside now and then, but the dances were packed every week!"

In fact, the dances at Bayfield were well attended from the day the first round-shaped dance pavilion was opened at the turn of the century on the Bayfield River. Tudor Marks was the builder - his hall eventually became a cottage which is still used, according to Ethel (Jowett) Poth, whose family has had a long association with Bayfield.

"William Jowett operated Jowett's Grove at The Point on the north side of the river," she writes. "There were cottages and picnic grounds in the park along the bank overlooking the lake. The first dance pavilion at Jowett's Grove was a frame building with coal oil lamps along the sides and a raised platform for the musicians at one end. In 1920, after William built a larger pavilion - also with a view of the lake - the frame one was razed and the materials were used to build cottage #17.

"This new pavilion had a wide screened-in verandah on the west and north sides where people could view the lake. Inside, a balcony allowed the spectators the pleasure of looking down at the dancers while listening to the music. At one time there was jitney dancing, and people could roam the beach or sit out in the picnic grounds between dances."

One of the popular bands Ethel remembers performing at the pavilion was led by Harold Skinner. "Harold on violin, plus piano, drums and saxophone - and we needed no expensive sound equipment. Evidently our ears were better in the 1920's! As time went on into the 1940's, the orchestras with their beat could be heard a mile away."

Constance Brown was born in 1905, and from ages nine to eighteen she spent the two summer months at Bayfield. She writes: "My family had a cottage in Lakeside Park on the south side of the river. On the north side Jowett's Grove had a beautiful dance pavilion and every Saturday night a group of us - mostly teenagers - would all troop over to the dance hall. We stopped at Mustard's Sawmill on the bridge for a hot dog - the best I've ever tasted. The hall was a big wooden building and had a balcony where our parents often sat and watched us dance - one orchestra I remember was Harold Skinner. Some people came by boat from Detroit up Lake Huron, stayed at a hotel and went to the pavilion. We children thought they were so sophisticated."

In 1960, Clinton businessman Red Garon decided to purchase the park from Lillian Jowett. Red's widow, Margaret, says that initially he did not have the time to operate his dry cleaning business in town as well as the dance pavilion, so he leased the building to the Scott family. "But after we married in 1964, Red and I took over full management of the park and pavilion, and moved into the grounds for the summer months," says Margaret. Red was very well-known in his community and liked by all who came in contact with him.

"One of the landmarks of Jowett's Grove was a huge red barn," describes Margaret. "There were eight or nine stalls on the lower level where picnickers in the old days would tie their horses and buggies for the day."

Red and Margaret decided to improve the property extensively during their tenure at Bayfield. "We upgraded the facility with sewers and roadways and it became a very popular tent and trailer camp," says Margaret. Red and I converted the barn into our living quarters upstairs, with a laundromat on the main level - the stalls were removed and a large card room was also built downstairs. Actually, the card nights became so popular that they were eventually moved to the dance hall. Of course the pavilion was the main attraction for both campers and the general public who came from miles around to dance."

A stairway with about 100 steps led down from the pavilion in Jowett's Grove to the beach, creating a very romantic setting for couples out on a moonlight stroll. The Garons landscaped the property extensively, removing masses of tangled vines so that the hundreds of tall trees could flourish.

This sketch of the dance pavilion at Jowett's Grove is the only visual reminder that Margaret Garon has of the days when she and her husband, Red, ran the park and the hall.

During the years previous to the Garon's ownership, Jowett's Grove had attracted bands from the local area as well as orchestras with international fame. Lionel Thornton, Tony Pastor and even the Lombardo Family Orchestra (in the early days) from London all played at Bayfield. Red and Margaret ran their dances on Wednesday and Saturday nights throughout the summer, opening on the traditional May 24th weekend and closing on Labour Day. As with most summer pavilions, there was no heat in the building. Their kids also became involved with the business, running the concession booth. The couple changed the pavilion's music policy to reflect the tastes of the kids; rock bands gradually replaced orchestras, and in the 1960's some of the largest crowds ever made their way to the Bayfield Pavilion.

The campground portion of the park never had an empty spot. "Every site was filled, many with regular campers who had seasonal spots - quite a bit of our business was with American tourists. And when the park was sold for development there were many disappointed guests who simply did not know where they would go."

As they were closing the park for the season in the mid 1980's, the Garons were approached in a rather casual manner by a lawyer who asked them if they would be interested in selling. "It was a very spur-of-the-moment decision for us," says Margaret, "and we decided on the spot to sell." The couple did stay at the park as patrons for a few years while Red continued his laundromat and dry-cleaning business in Clinton.

"We were saddened when the park was closed down a few years later for a housing development," says Margaret. The familiar red barn was demolished, as was the dance pavilion where thousands of dancers had created their special memories at Bayfield. The beautiful trees under which people camped, walked and danced are also gone - the developer completely levelled the property to facilitate lot division and construction. In 1995 many of the lots were still for sale.

There is still a Jowett's Grove cottage rental business at Bayfield, not far from the site of the old park, a reminder in name only of the summer dances that used to take place at the Bayfield Pavilion.

Chapter Ten

GRAND BEND - LAKEVIEW CASINO

Saturday, June 6, 1981, was one of the most memorable occasions ever celebrated in the community of Grand Bend on Lake Huron. It was billed as 'Eric McIlroy Day,' in honour of the late businessman who owned and operated Lakeview Casino for 30 years. He was a pillar of the town; as a member of many associations including a stint on local Council he was one of the driving forces guiding the growth of Grand Bend, nurturing it from a small holiday destination to a major summer resort with a large year-round population.

The events of June 6 may just be a memory today in the minds of those who attended the celebrations, but there is one significant physical reminder of that outstanding day. At the southeast corner of Highways 81 and 21, a lovingly crafted fieldstone cairn with a bronze plaque was unveiled by the former Lieutenant Governor of Ontario, the honourable Pauline McGibbon. In the

centre of the tastefully designed plaque is a carved likeness of Eric McIlroy, surrounded by the logos of the organizations he formed, led and/or belonged - the Village Council, Lions Club, Chamber of Commerce, the Mocha Temple Shrine and the Ontario Harness Horseman's Association. The engraved message is simple, but sums up the contribution he made to Grand Bend: 'In Tribute to W. Eric McIlroy whose Lakeview Casino brought joy and music to thousands. Grand Bend remembers!'

Twenty-five days later, on July 1, 1981, the dance hall that Eric's father-in-law built in 1919 was destroyed by fire.

When Lakeview Casino went up in smoke, part of the soul of Grand Bend was lost. Like so many lakeside towns that overflow with summer sun-seekers in July and August, the pavilion was the hub of the beach. In the case of Lakeview Casino, its location made it the major focal point of Grand Bend, being situated on the beach at the very end of the town's main street. Whether you swam, sunbathed, wandered about or simply drove down the main drag, Lakeview Casino was the largest and most prominent building.

And on dance night there was nowhere else to go but Lakeview! From opening night with the then-unknown Lombardo brothers, to Rudy Vallee, to the Big Bands of the 1930's & 40's, right up to rock acts of the 1970's, Lakeview Casino booked in the biggest names in the business for special one-night engagements. It was also the local bands from Ontario who provided the steady danceable music that made the warm summer nights so enchanting for dancers.

The town of Grand Bend can trace its early beginnings back to about 1830 when it was originally an isolated lumbering town, known under a variety of names, all relating to 'meeting place.' Finally, the name Grand Bend was coined after the sharp turn in the Ausable River which flows through the area.

Building a dance pavilion at Grand Bend was the brainchild of George and Ida Eccleston back in 1916. A grocer from London, Ontario, George and his wife purchased a huge 45-acre parcel of land owned by the Levitt family, extending from the lake all the way back to the present main intersection of the highways. The cost: $9100, which at the time was a fairly hefty sum of money. George was intent on constructing a dance pavilion and decided to set up a temporary platform protected by canvas - really a dancing tent.

Opening night was July 1, 1917, with the Lombardo family from London performing at the official opening ceremony later that month, billed as the 'London Italian Orchestra.' Some say that this was the Lombardos' first paid job, when they received $10 for their efforts. Others claim that the first remuneration the group received ($10 - the going rate, it seems) was at the Delaware Town Hall in the summer of 1917. In any case, when this original version of the Lombardo family orchestra was just in its infancy - during the summer of 1917 with the Great War still raging in Europe - the members of the band likely had no idea of the decades of success that lay before them.

The original Lakeview Pavilion opened on July 25 1917, featuring the London Italian Orchestra who would later become internationally famous as the Lombardo Brothers.

Well, anyone who has camped in stormy weather will attest to the fact that tents are not the best form of protection; George soon realized that his dance tent was no match for the summer storms that periodically blew in off Lake Huron, so he and Ida decided to build a larger and more solid dance pavilion, converting the first platform into a picnic shelter. A baseball diamond was built beside the shelter and became the site of many friendly competitions.

Lakeview Casino was built to last, constructed with wood, and concrete which George poured himself. Materials were hauled to the lakefront by horse-drawn wagons. Two years after his first platform, George and Ida officially

Two years later, in 1919, George Eccleston opened his new pavilion (above), pouring the cement himself. The original hall was converted into a picnic shelter, seen in the lower photo.

opened the new dance pavilion in 1919. Success was immediate, as seasonal residents made their way from nearby cottages and lodges, and permanent residents arrived any way they could - by foot, horse and carriage or automobile. After building the pavilion, George and Ida opened a few small novelty shops and a bath house underneath the dance hall.

During the 1920's George devoted his efforts beyond his casino as he spearheaded projects to improve Grand Bend itself. He put in sidewalks, paved Main Street and other streets as well, which were eventually turned over to the village, and he encouraged other business people to come to the Bend and set up shop to cater to the increasing number of summer visitors. Grand Bend was quickly being recognized as a prime holiday spot.

Grand Bend enjoyed the benefit of being close to major Ontario cities like London and Sarnia and even Windsor, but was also able to draw substantial numbers of people from the U.S., who crossed at nearby border points. This proximity to the States also made it possible for George to book in bands that might have thought twice about travelling too far into the hinterland of Ontario (although Gerry Dunn in Bala would later astonish dancers by bringing big names into Muskoka). Bands and entertainers could easily fit a job at Grand Bend into their itinerary as they toured across the southern part of the province.

Lakeview Casino featured jitney dancing from the early days up until the early 1940's.

Some of the early bands to play the hall were McKinney's Cotton Pickers and McKinney's Chocolate Dandies - two black bands from Detroit who were immensely popular wherever they played, both in the States and Canada. Emerson Gill, Ted Burt's Nine Royal Collegians, Brian Farnan and his Boys, Gene Fritzley and Fred Elliott's Orchestra also played during the 1920's and 30's. Two surviving members of Fred's band shared their recollections of the Casino in letters to me.

Writes George Cairns: "I well remember the dance pavilions. In fact, I played in some of them during the period 1931-1935, as a member of the Fred Elliott Orchestra. This group was based in Hamilton, mostly from McMaster University (though I was an 'outsider' from U. of T. Engineering). We played in 1931 at Southampton, followed in '32 and '33 in a very large pavilion at Grand Bend, where we followed by about five years a band from London, Ontario - Guy Lombardo! In 1934 and '35 we played the pavilion at Orillia and finished in September, 1935 at the Silver Slipper in Toronto. Then the band broke up as all the members had completed their college courses. I have many fond memories of these pavilions as well as many others where we were able to play one-nighter stands in the pre-season in May and June."

Art Duncan sent a picture of the Fred Elliott Orchestra, taken in Grand Bend, and echoes similar words to George: "We started out with a seven-man group playing in the pavilion at Southampton. The next year we added two men and spent the next two summers at Grand Bend. The following year we added another man and played a couple of years at the Couchiching Park Pavilion in Orillia. We had a lot of fun - there were a lot of good bands around then."

Softball games, parachute leaps into the lake and Fred Elliott's band brought people to Grand Bend for this July 1st celebration. Midnight Frolics on long summer weekends allowed hall owners to run dances that began just after 12 a.m. Ontario laws prohibited dancing on Sundays.

In 1931, tragedy struck Ida Eccleston's life when she lost George to complications from diabetes. She was faced with a major decision: sell the business, or continue to run the pavilion herself with the assistance of her daughter, Ella. Ida chose to keep Lakeview Casino in her hands, a move which would ultimately benefit both her family, and on a larger scale, Grand Bend itself.

Ella married Eric McIlroy the following year, and one would expect that Eric would naturally want to step in to his late father-in-law's shoes and operate the hall. Not so. Eric had just embarked upon a promising career with Eaton's in Toronto where the couple was living (Ella worked at Lakeview during the summer) and he did not wish to leave a secure job to run a dance pavilion.

Eric had been born in Belfast, Ireland, in 1909 where he apprenticed in the textile business. After moving to Toronto in 1928 he joined Eaton's in the purchasing department and met Ella during her winter sojourn in the city. Eric and George barely had a chance to become acquainted before George died, a fact that Ella once said was too bad - she feels they would have been good friends.

Five years after marrying Ella, in 1937, Eric changed his mind when Ida asked the couple if they would be interested in purchasing Lakeview Casino from her. This turning point in the history of the hall would mark the beginning of a new life in Grand Bend for Ella and Eric which would eventually lead to the McIlroys being called 'Grand Bend's Mr. and Mrs. Music.'

LAKEVIEW CASINO
TO: **ELLA** AND **ERIC McELROY**
GRAND BEND'S — "MR. AND MRS. MUSIC"
GREAT BANDS! GREAT MUSIC!

From 1937 until they sold Lakeview in 1966, Eric and Ella worked long days every summer, operating a number of businesses underneath the hall during the day, and running the dances at night.

The Big Band era was in full swing when Eric came on board, and he seemed to have the knack of combining his people skills with the enjoyment of being an impresario. He brought the people what they wanted - the best entertainment of the period in a relaxed holiday setting on one of Ontario's prime beach resorts. Along with stars like Tommy Dorsey and Louis Armstrong, Canadian music greats were featured every summer. Jimmy Namaro on his famous xylophone was a favourite, as were Juliette, Ellis McLintock, the Modernaires (with Fred Davis on trumpet), Stan Patton, Bert Niosi, Len Hopkins, Joan Fairfax ... the list is long. With London being so close to Grand Bend, many of this city's best orchestras appeared at Lakeview, including Neil McKay, Bobby Downs and Lionel Thornton.

To honour Eric and Ella McIlroy's policy of hiring musicians belonging to the Union, and running a first-rate hall, the couple was presented with a special citation from the Musicians' Local 279 in 1965. Few operators were lucky enough to be so honoured - Emmett and Pat McGrath who ran Port Elgin's Cedar Crescent Casino received a similar award three years later.

As a patron in the 1930's, Frank Sills has a couple of hilarious stories to tell. "The pavilion in Grand Bend was a mecca for all the young people in our area as well as many from the U.S. who spent their summer at the Bend. It was a wonderful ; it had a beautiful floor with a wide walk space all around it, elevated about ten feet with a wide set of steps leading up to the entrance where an attendant wouldn't let anyone in unless they were suitably dressed in jacket, tie and trousers - no shorts allowed. There was always a first-class band - one I remember was Jimmy Namaro with his xylophone."

Jimmy Namaro, renowned xylophonist, posed for this picture on the beach at Grand Bend.

"In 1939 I went out there with a friend from town. A dreamy waltz tune was playing and he was dancing with a girl much shorter than him, so he was sort of draped over her. At the conclusion of the dance he came back to me and said, 'Am I ever embarrassed. All the time we were dancing I never noticed that I was keeping time to the music by plucking on her brassiere strap.' 'Did she object?', I asked. 'No.' 'So what are you worried about?'

"Another episode happened in 1940 with another friend who had enlisted in the air force and was acting as a Drogue operator (the person in an aircraft who lets out a target on the end of a long rope from the rear of the plane so that other planes have something to shoot at). I couldn't get my Dad's car for the dance but my brother had an old Whippet coupe that he had made into a truck. We set out and after about three miles our front wheels turned in towards each other because of a broken radius tie rod. We returned at a slow pace because my pal had to walk in front and continually kick the wheels straight while I drove.

"Next day I got the trouble fixed and we headed out to the dance. Everything went okay - a great dancing night and my friend in his air force uniform (I joined the forces later in the year). At the beginning of the second last dance he came to me and asked if we could leave right away. When I asked him why he said, 'While dancing with the last girl I told her that I was a bush pilot who came down from the North in a Cadillac. I just didn't want her to see us getting into that old wreck of yours.' So the old line-shooting was catching up to him!"

Eric's generosity and community spirit quickly became obvious to the area through the many local organizations and causes he helped out at Lakeview. During the War 'Tip' Tipping gave a benefit concert with proceeds going to the Canadian Wartime Board, the Modernaires played for the same cause and later for the Canadian Red Cross British Bomb Victims Fund. The Casino was also used for many other fundraising events. When Dutch immigrants needed a place to hold Mass, Eric volunteered Lakeview for their Sunday morning services in 1947, '48, and '49.

Through the mid-1950's and into the '60's Grand Bend was enjoying glorious days of summer fun. Beach parties, beauty contests, hootenanys all brought out enthusiastic crowds and Lakeview Casino was always front and centre at these events. Dance music was played almost every night, particularly in the 50's. Eric and Ella were also well aware

GOOD NEWS!

IT IS COMING — The Famous Band That ENDURES and Gets More Popular Each Year

Enlarged this Season to 11 Men
With Pinkey Hunter and Extra Entertainers

Direct From BAMBOO GARDENS   **W.T.A.M. RADIO**

EMERSON GILL

and his Famous
DANCE ORCHESTRA

Mr. Gill this year is not only playing the popular numbers, but dance hits from the notable Broadway shows and the celebrated theme songs of the talking pictures.

THIS IS THE SAME BAND WHICH BROADCASTS AS THE **FOX FUR TRAPPERS** AND HAS ACHIEVED A NATIONAL CHAIN RADIO REPUTATION

GRAND BEND
ONE NIGHT ONLY

TUES., AUG. 13th

ADMISSION 25c.   ---   DANCING 4 for 25c.

Free - Free
GRAND BEND CASINO
MODERN
– AND –
OLD-TIME DANCING
MONDAY, JUNE 13

In order to introduce this new policy of special nights for Old-Time dancing, the management of the casino invites you to be their guests at *no* charge whatever.

HEMMING'S ORCHESTRA
Come out for one grand time.
- ALL FREE -

LAKEVIEW CASINO
GRAND BEND
Opening
Dances
SATURDAY, MAY 22nd
AND
MIDNIGHT, MAY 23rd
Neil McKay's All-Star Orchestra

☀ RUDY VALLEE ☀
APPEARING AT
GRAND BEND CASINO
FRIDAY, AUGUST 29th

Lakeview Casino
Grand Bend
VARIETY CONCERT
The Modernaires Orchestra

and Guest Artists
The Sunshine Boys, Gerald and Leon Paul, Comedians. Winners of Ken Soble's Toronto-Montreal Radio contests.
Anna Mae Luft, 10 year old Violin Virtuoso. Gold medalist and winner of Marson Scholarship
Fred Funk, Chime Soloist and Xylophonist. Star of Variety Entertainers and Musical Mountaineers

Sunday, August 16th, 1942
9 p.m.

Every artist donating his services and travelling expenses entirely free of charge——all proceeds for

Canadian Red Cross British Bomb Victims Fund

Lakeview Casino
GRAND BEND
Summer Season
Opening
Saturday, June 25
DANCING
Every Night
BILL JUPP AND HIS ORCHESTRA

Goodwill Concerts
EACH SUNDAY 9 P.M.
Starting June 26.
Clarence Petrie
and his
RADIO NIGHT HAWKS
Sponsored by The Grand Bend Lions Club.

Brian Farnan played Lakeview Casino in 1934.

Len Hopkins' bus enabled the band to tour in comfort. It's parked in front of Lakeview.

Eric McIlroy with singer Joyce Hahn.

that music was changing, and they decided to bring in some rock 'n' roll acts for the kids. Many rock groups from London and other Ontario towns and cities looked forward to playing a job at Grand Bend, where they would arrive early enough in the day to enjoy the sand and surf before hopping up on stage for the evening's performance.

Eric McIlroy was never satisfied to simply run the Casino; he was a natural organizer and jumped in feet-first wherever he felt he could make a difference. As far back as 1950 he was one of the chief organizers of the Grand Bend Lions Club and became the first President. The annual Lions dance was always held at Lakeview, with a star brought in as entertainment.

When the first village council was established in Grand Bend, Eric was elected in 1951. He finished the 1952 term and was re-elected in 1957 and '58.

Through his expertise in promotion and public relations it was not surprising to see Eric as the chairman of the Grand Bend Promotion committee in 1956. This organization was the forerunner of the Chamber of Commerce, of which Eric became the first President.

When the South Huron Hospital board was formed in nearby Exeter, Eric's abilities and skills were appreciated as a founding member. He remained on the hospital board after it opened in 1954 and continued to serve through 1965. Eric was also on the board when the Grand Bend Medical Centre was built in 1971.

He was made a lifetime member of the Bluewater Shriners in the 1960's.

As a person who developed a keen interest in harness horse racing, Eric became a member of the Ontario Harness Horse Association and was a director from 1964 to 1968.

With his interests so widely spread, Eric and Ella felt that it might be time to consider selling Lakeview Casino, but continue to run the Sun and Surf Shops on the lower level. Once the decision had been made, the business was put up for sale in 1966. Bob McWilliams from Windsor took over the

Grand Bend beach
those busy days —
the 50's and 60's

Appearing one night only...

THE
ONE
AND
ONLY
Louis
Armstrong

America's Number One Musical Ambassador

LAKEVIEW CASINO
GRAND BEND

Friday, July 20   9:00 p.m. — 1:00 a.m.

TICKETS $5.00 EACH — ON SALE AT THE BOX OFFICE AND VILLAGE SHOP, SUN SHOP, AND SURF SHOP

A Highlight of Your Summer, Whether You Come to Dance or Just to Listen. The
Opportunity of a Life-Time to Meet and Talk to Satchmo

Intermission Dancing Music By . . .

Ron Brown and His Orchestra —   FEATURING JACK
LEVY — VOCALIST

Top - original dance floor of Casino was railed off for jitney dancing.
Below - renovated interior with new stage.

operation with the intention of creating a larger all-purpose meeting, banquet and convention facility that could be used year-round. This fizzled as the business changed hands to Dennis Calder who ran into financial difficulties. Tim Fraleigh eventually assumed ownership, making a number of changes to Lakeview including the addition of a large pinball arcade and wax museum. It was under Fraleigh's possession that disaster struck Grand Bend's jewel.

When flames broke out at Lakeview Casino on July 1, 1981, three local fire brigades rushed to the pavilion, but it was obvious that their job would simply be one of containing the blaze. Arson was the likely cause since the fire had its origins in more than one location in the building. A fire the previous week had caused about $145,000 damage to some of the businesses in the lower level of Lakeview Casino, including a couple of fast food places, a kite and frisbee shop and the pinball arcade. The second blaze ensured that the pavilion was finished off completely, and even threatened the nearby home and businesses of Nick Carter. The fire was extinguished by the early morning hours, but the damage was devastating and final - only the concrete walls remained, the walls George Eccleston poured 62 years previously.

In a 1981 article Ella McIlroy is quoted as saying, "I wasn't surprised to see the walls still standing after the blaze because they were made with my dad's own two hands." Ella McIlroy also once said, "My dad had great visions and Eric was able to carry some of those out." Eric McIlroy had died on November 4, 1979.

June 6, 1981, saw many of the people who had been touched in some way by Eric McIlroy pay tribute to him. Business people, musicians, politicians and friends all turned out for the unveiling of the plaque and the evening dance that followed. Music for the dance was supplied by Lionel Thornton's Casa Royal Orchestra. Lionel was also the Master of Ceremonies for the day, a most fitting choice since Lionel's orchestra was a regular on Lakeview Casino's stage.

Grand Bend's Lakeview Casino.

The dance pavilion

Grand Bend remembers Eric McIlroy

Times-Advocate

Boy from Belfast, Ireland makes his name in Grand Bend

SATURDAY, JUNE 6, 1981

JOIN US IN CELEBRATING W. ERIC McILROY DAY
- UNVEILING OF PLAQUE AND CAIRN
AT CENTENNIAL PARK (CORNER OF 81 & 21 HWYS.) AT 3 P.M.

Unveiling by Honourable Pauline McGibbon

- DANCING BEGINNING AT 9 P.M. AND MIDNIGHT BUFFET
AT HURON COUNTRY PLAYHOUSE SATURDAY, JUNE 6

Dancing 9.00 - 1.00   Tickets $33.00 each

FEATURING
Lionel Thornton's Casa Royal Orchestra
under the direction of Grayden Hopkins

Music and memories at Lakeview Casino

Grand Bend hosted many big bands

Music rose from beach that hugged Grand Bend

Lakeview Casino attracted thousands over five decades

ERIC McILROY
Salute to an exceptional person

W. Eric McIlroy Memorial Trust
MEMBERSHIP CONTRIBUTION CARD
Grand Bend Remembers! I Remember Too!

Lakeview Casino— brought joy and music to thousands

Since the 1981 tribute, the original Lakeview Casino site remains simply a vast sandy expanse on the shore of Lake Huron. A billboard advertised the land not long ago as 'Lakeview Casino Development Site Available For Sale or Joint Venture,' but it may be some time before another building rises from the beach. The land is privately owned and is currently being used as a parking lot. One fact is almost certain - there will never be another dance pavilion here, just as there will never be another Eric McIlroy.

Chapter Eleven

IPPERWASH CASINO

Long before the days of Ipperwash Provincial Park and the ensuing 1995 conflict over land claims in the area, the Casino at Ipperwash Beach was the centre of social life for many summers.

Jeanette Ovens' husband, John, has a direct connection with this pavilion. She writes: "My husband's uncle, Stuart Ovens built the Ipperwash Casino at Ipperwash Beach on Lake Huron in 1929, approximately 50 miles from London. Although John was just a small boy he remembers spending summers at the Ovens' cottages across the road from the Casino. To the best of his knowledge he believes dances were held nearly every night of the week at that time. The Casino and hotel were two different establishments.

"Not being old enough to wait on customers, it was his job to sweep the floors and do some of the odd jobs. The Casino was destroyed by fire a number of years ago."

London musician Jim Steele played here with the John Brenan Band and recalls the pavilion as being very popular during July and August.

Johnny Brenan and His Orchestra.

Chapter Twelve

SARNIA AND AREA

Sarnia - Kenwick Terrace
Bright's Grove - Kenwick-on-the-Lake

The name Jack Kennedy evokes strong memories in many of Sarnia's residents. Jack was known by everyone as The Music Man, and for good reason. Jack was not only a talented musician and orchestra leader, he also owned Sarnia's two largest and most popular dance venues, Kenwick Terrace in downtown Sarnia, and the romantic Kenwick-on-the-Lake in Bright's Grove. Both halls brought the biggest entertainers in the business to Sarnia. The music store he founded in 1966 - today operated by son Douglas - continues to bear his name. Jack was both a sharp businessman and a generous citizen who was most satisfied when his music gave people pleasure.

Doug expands on his father's musical talent. "Dad was an exceptional musician who could read music fluently or play by ear when necessary; he could also arrange music quickly, even tunes that he had heard just once on the radio. Other than strings, Dad was proficient on all musical instruments including piano, sax, other woodwinds and horns; he played in orchestras from the time he was 14 until he turned 44."

Genevieve Kennedy also says that her husband was a great arranger. "He wasn't keen on small combos, but loved big bands," she says. Jack led his own 10-piece band which featured a female vocalist. In his early days as a musician Jack had three orchestras and travelled throughout southern Ontario performing at various pavilions. For example, he would play two days at Collins Bay, move on to Hamilton for two more dates and then play the remainder of the week in

Sarnia. Jack's orchestra also performed for dances throughout Lambton county, including places such as Wallaceburg's Primrose Gardens, The Pyranon in Chatham and of course at his own dance halls.

Jack Kennedy's Dance Band performed throughout Ontario.

"Dad always worked extremely hard and threw himself into every aspect of his work, whether it was music, business or physical work on his buildings," says Doug. The Sarnia man was well-liked by everyone who met him, and he made a point of taking time both to talk and to make music, just to perk up a person's day. For instance, during the summer when he would be working away at his beloved Kenwick-On-The-Lake, Jack would take time to play a few tunes on his piano for the CGIT girls every day as they walked by the pavilion on their way to the variety store.

DANCE
PRIMROSE GARDENS
WALLACEBURG
WEDNESDAY
OCTOBER 22ND
JACK KENNEDY'S
DANCE BAND
Dancing   Admission
9.30 to 1.30   50c each
"God Save The King"

Before Kenwick-on-the-Lake, Jack and Gen had operated the Starlite Gardens (later to become the Rose Gardens), an outdoor dance venue , and rented the Bayview Park Dance Pavilion. When the weatherman called for rain, the dance moved from Starlite to Bayview. "I often helped carry band equipment over to Bayview during rainy nights," says Gen. Due to a large swampy area in a nearby park, Starlite Gardens was continually infested with mosquitoes, alleviated only by burning many smudge pots which were carried around by the staff. One particular musician - saxophonist Sammy Lang - was so bothered by these pesky critters that he soaked his socks in the repellant to keep the bugs away.

Previous to Jack and Genevieve building Kenwick-on-the-Lake, they had already gained a number of years experience in the business, having opened Kenwick Terrace in Sarnia in 1943. The name 'Kenwick' was derived by combining part of Jack's last name with Gen's, which was Warwick. As the name suggests, Gen worked with Jack as an equal partner in their businesses.

The building which eventually became home to Kenwick Terrace in downtown Sarnia was purchased by Jack and Gen in early 1943. Originally called St. Andrews Hall after the church across the road which ran Saturday night dances, the facility was later transformed into a roller rink and then became home to the Lambton Ford dealership. After this last tenant vacated the premises, the upstairs hall required a great deal of renovating to transform it into a grand dance hall. "The car dealership used to store extra vehicles upstairs, so they had removed a large portion of the ceiling to build a ramp," says Doug. "Unfortunately, oil and various other fluids from the cars had leaked onto the floor, so it had to be completely restored."

Louis Armstrong officially opened Kenwick Terrace on January 31, 1943.

Kenwick Terrace held regular dances with Jack's group, and booked in internationally known orchestras and singers regularly. The hall also served as a large banquet facility, accommodating up to 800 people. Doug started working at Kenwick Terrace as a young lad, scraping plates and working in the coat check.

Weekly shows were broadcast across Canada on the CBC Radio network, and William Boyd remembers those programs. "Cy Strange was a singer with the Jack Kennedy Orchestra," he writes. "Cy went on to become a figure at CBC radio after his singing days were completed."

Kenwick Terrace was operated by Jack and Gen until 1978 when the couple decided to demolish the building and erect a large apartment/office complex. Jack's business acumen was evident over the years as he purchased surrounding properties; by the time he was ready to tear down the old building, he owned a significant block of land. Jack was also instrumental in developing a major downtown mall area in Strathroy, a few miles to the east of Sarnia. "Mom and Dad had an excellent business relationship," says Doug. "Dad was shrewd, and very generous, but all major decisions were a joint effort."

Gen says that she and Jack were the first to bring Guy Lombardo and his orchestra back to Canada. "Prior to that he had been appearing only in the United States because of a contract that made it unprofitable to play in Canada. When the contract expired, he came to our hall first."

Lawrence Welk became a friend of the Kennedys, even though his first appearance lost them money at Kenwick Terrace. "His music was beautiful, but he was unknown at the time. He became a good friend of the family and we visited with him in California. Welk did have a good time cooking up hamburgers after the performance, though," recalls Gen.

On the other hand, Tommy Dorsey was very demanding. "He even made sure that he left the performance 15 minutes before the show was over to avoid having to meet his fans and sign autographs," says Gen.

Kenwick Terrace in downtown Sarnia was a multi-functional hall
with Big Band dances and banquets keeping the staff busy.

Kenwick Terrace ran full tilt from September to June. "We did all the proms from the area, including many from the States, and ran a large catering business as well," says Gen. Jack would often provide dinner music on the organ in the hall. Many local people found part-time employment at Kenwick Terrace, and full-time work at the summer venue. "We'd hire students from Western University in London and they would stay in the staff quarters attached to the hall."

Bill and Elizabeth Baldock have pleasant memories of Kenwick Terrace. "Many an evening was enjoyed with our friends here," writes Bill. "The flexible wooden dance floor allowed you to dance all night to the sounds of pop, jazz, big name bands and local ones such as Jack Kennedy, Johnie Bonds and the Rhythm Ramblers. Years later our oldest son Jeff, along with his friends John Robins and Wayne Orton worked as bus boys at Kenwick Terrace. I proposed to my wife at Kenwick-on-the-Lake 37 years ago. Les Brown and His Band of Renown were playing that warm summer evening on the shore of Lake Huron."

As Bill describes, the location of Kenwick-on-the-Lake makes this hall perhaps the most memorable for people who came here to dance. Although Kenwick Terrace was Jack and Gen's primary business, when the opportunity arose to acquire such a unique location, they decided it was a worthwhile risk, and would be an ideal seasonal alternative to their downtown hall. With their experience in running dances at Starlite Gardens, operating a summer hall of their own would be a logical move.

Grace Schultz supplies the background which led to Kenwick-on-the-Lake. "Crinnians ran an informal dance hall nearby named Crinnians Grove, covered with a roof and surrounded with barbed wire. Bands were brought in, although there was not much of a stage on which to set up." After the War, Jack Kennedy could see the potential for building a large, well-run dance operation on the Crinnians location, so he purchased it and drew up plans to build what was to become Kenwick-on-the-Lake, Sarnia-Lambton's most famous dancing landmark in its time.

Gen picks up the story. "We purchased the pavilion at Bright's Grove in March of 1946, with the first dance scheduled for June 16 of the same year." During those three months Jack drove all over southwestern Ontario sourcing down building supplies, scrounging materials from lumber and building yards to get the project off the ground. "After the War this material was difficult to find," explains Gen. All the cement acquired from suppliers was dyed red. Opening night was a culmination of a busy few weeks working with a designer and a builder - Walter Herridge - who fulfilled his promise to have it ready on schedule.

The grand opening included a visit from Canada's Governor General. That June evening marked the beginning of a summer dancing tradition that lasted well into the 1950's for Jack Kennedy and his band.

Kenwick-on-the-Lake was popular for its outdoor terrazzo dance floor which Jack had enlarged and improved. There was also an indoor hardwood floor. The family planted trees, rock gardens, opened two dining rooms and a hairdressing salon. "Everything we made was re-invested back into Kenwick-on-the-Lake," says Gen.

The couple improved the picnic grounds which were right on the water beside a huge beach. "We opened a bathhouse and stand to rent bathing suits, and then opened a concession booth - it wasn't unusual to sell over 1,000 hot dogs on a summer Sunday," says Gen. They built an outdoor bowling alley, set up small shops and installed rides for the kids. "The popcorn machine ran non-stop during those busy summer days."

Jack painted the building a pastel pink, and applied a new coat every year to keep it looking fresh and clean. Other than on New Year's Eve in Kenwick Terrace, booze was not allowed in the Kennedy's halls, a rule that they insisted upon. "We drew from all over Ontario and nearby towns in the U.S.," says Gen. The season ran until Labour Day.

Memories still strong of showplace

In its hayday it was perhaps Sarnia-Lambton's most famo

Kenwick-on-th the big band era t during the late 1

Even today, th memories from t danced up a stor

For the man wl memories are stil

Jack Kennedy War era, when he showplace.

Building mate says. But he was forming showpla western Ontario, lumber and build the ground.

he had the Kenwick-on-the-Lake constructed

and claimed their spots on the dance floor. Un

KENWICK on the LAKE
"Canada's Finest Dance Paladium"

Kenwick-on-the-Lake
Canada's Newest Amusement Wonder

Presents IN PERSON

ART KASSEL
XXXX
AND HIS
"Kassels in the Air"
ORCHESTRA

TUESDAY, AUGUST 27th, 1946

Advance Sale $1.50   Regular Admission $1.75

"Weaver of Melodies"
Popular Song Writer—Leader
Music Corporation of America
Presents

IN PERSON
ART
KASSEL
and his
"KASSELS IN
THE AIR"

Kenwick-on-the-Lake floated with music

Closed dance pavilion holds romantic memories

One of the reasons the crowds were so large at Kenwick-on-the-Lake was that many people rented cottages nearby for periods of usually two weeks. "So you see, there was a regular turnover of people," says Gen. Dancers were given a black light stamp so they could take a stroll around the picnic grounds during the evening.

Don Messer was the first country act to perform at Kenwick. Not being big fans of country music, Jack and Gen were leery about hiring this "fiddler from down East," but were amazed when people lined up hours early to see their idol.

"Vaughn Monroe thought that Kenwick-on-the-Lake was the most beautiful place he had ever played," says Gen. Norm Harris played for one summer with his band and enjoyed the experience so much that he returned the following year by himself to sing with the band.

Dancing took place on most nights except Monday when wrestling was a big draw under the stars. Mass was held on Sunday in the enclosed dance hall.

Jack and Gen's days at Kenwick-on-the-Lake began at 6 a.m. and often did not end until 2 a.m. That was one reason they decided to sell the business in 1951. Kenwick-on-the-Lake was eventually sold back to the original landowner who was allowed to retain the name. "Jack was a real do-it-yourself type of individual," says Gen. It was not unusual for business associates to call on Jack to discuss matters, only to find him with his sleeves rolled up in the middle of a plumbing repair.

Grace Schultz says, "The real success of this operation were during Jack and Gen's time, as well as the years the next owners ran the operation. This period would be from 1946 until 1962." By this time the big band era had really given way to smaller combos and rock music was fully entrenched as the more popular music form. After 1962 the building fell into significant disrepair, and had changed hands once again. Fire had destroyed the bandstand, and the complex was in a sad state of deterioration. Between 1966 and 1969 a group of younger people rented the facility and tried to revive the hall by introducing rock music, but even this new format was not very successful.

Jack directed his love for music into the retail business in the 1960's. "Dad had been the top producing rep in the area for Heintzman, and eventually opened his own music store in Sarnia, specializing in pianos and organs," says Doug, who continues to run the business founded in 1966, still bearing his late father's name. In order to promote his music store, Jack worked the local malls with his electric organ, and his performances of Christmas music became an annual tradition that many Sarnia residents still recall. It's also a tradition that Doug has continued.

When the first electric organ arrived in Lambton County, it was no surprise that Jack Kennedy was the proud owner of this instrument. He later became his church's organist, a position he held for 15 years, never taking a dime for payment. Jack also had the opportunity to purchase a piano that had been used for years in Massey Hall. Today the historic instrument sits in quiet splendour in the large living room of the family home, overlooking the St. Clair River.

Outside of music, one of the loves of Jack's life was boating; Gen still owns the 43-foot yacht they acquired years ago - it's moored in the family's boathouse. In fact, Jack enjoyed his music so much that he had an organ installed on the deck of his yacht, effectively combining his passion for music with his favourite hobby. Wherever the couple docked for the night, Jack would crank up the instrument to entertain anybody who was nearby. One of Jack's favourite ports of call was up the Lake Huron coast in Port Elgin where people still remember Jack playing tunes on the organ at dockside. "Those impromptu sing-songs, dances and concerts are memories that I'll carry with me all my life," says Gen.

Astute, musical, generous, well-liked ... Jack Kennedy was all of these and more. When The Music Man passed away a few years ago, the city of Sarnia lost a little piece of its heart.

Rose Gardens

October 14th is a day when Dick and Elsie Rose usually pause for a moment and think back to the years when they ran Sarnia's most popular roller rink and dance hall - Rose Gardens. The final dance at their successful business was held October 14, 1974, drawing over 2,000 people who came out to enjoy one last evening at their favourite hall.

Dick and Elsie moved from London in 1951 to purchase the Starlite Gardens, an outdoor facility that featured dancing under the stars during the 1930's and 40's. It had been owned by the Kennedy family, who operated other successful businesses in Sarnia. Starlite Gardens was also called Parkside for a short period of time, due to its proximity to the large Canatara City Park, to the east of the hall.

Dick wanted to establish a roller skating rink but the dance floor was simply too small, so he immediately enlarged and re-surfaced the outdoor venue to 90 by 150 feet, which they re-named Rose Gardens. Dick and Elsie opened the club nightly and often held dances on the outdoor floor. They also operated a bakery on the premises which included a doughnut shop, the first of its kind in Sarnia. The Roses provided their special doughnuts, called 'spudnuts,' to the local high schools. Skaters could also buy a drink or ice cream for a dime, and a hot dog or fires for 15 cents.

"We could see the demand from the kids for year-round roller skating and dancing, so in 1961 we completely enclosed the rink and opened every night during the year," says Dick. Crowds of up to 1800 were not unusual for an evening of roller skating and dancing afterwards. Since he wanted to have a good selection of music suitable for the skaters, Dick purchased all the records to be played for the skating portion of the night. "I made a point of listening to each record in the store before I actually bought it."

YEAR ROUND
ENTERTAINMENT

- Dancing
- Roller Skating
- Record Hops
- Top Name Bands During the Summer Months

ROSE GARDENS

CANATARA PARK   337-2585   POINT EDWARD

Sarnia kids came to dance and roller skate at Rose Gardens.

The couple, along with their daughter Marilyn, held many Muscular Dystrophy fund-raising events and were presented numerous awards for their dedication to this cause. Dick and Elsie are particularly proud of a letter sent to them from entertainer Steve Allen for their participation in the cause. During fund-raising events, up to three bands would donate their time and the kids would receive special pins or brooches to signify that they had donated to the fund.

Record hops and dances with live bands were very popular during the 1950's and 60's. During the weekends skating would take place from 7 to 9:30 p.m., and then dancing would continue until midnight. Dick often held down the post as disc jockey, or on an especially busy evening Jerry Daniels, formerly of CHOK, would host the evenings. Occasional live broadcasts were done from Rose Gardens.

Dick recalls the night that Ronnie Hawkins was booked for a dance. "At the time he hadn't been in Canada for long and was not known in Sarnia. The young people didn't seem interested enough to come in and dance to his music, so we decided to run roller skating instead. So, Ronnie Hawkins played for skating that evening!"

Many other Canadian name artists played at the Rose Gardens, including Bobby Curtola, David Clayton Thomas (who went on to fame with Blood, Sweat and Tears) and The Staccatos (later the Five Man Electrical Band). Del Shannon played in place of Roy Orbison who had to cancel his gig at the last minute. Local bands were hired for regular dances and included The Volcanoes, The Capers and Jays Raiders.

The Roses decided to wind down the dancing portion in the late 60's because, as Elsie notes, "Skating events were much easier to control."

They had very strict rules on behaviour, which was a relief for parents who knew their kids were in good hands with the Roses. Says Dick: "If anyone did get out of line, the punishment was a two-week banishment, and since the Rose Gardens was the meeting place for young people, that was a penalty that no-one wanted to receive."

Above, Dick and Elsie Rose (right) were active in raising funds for Muscular Dystrophy. Below, the building was donated to the County of Lambton in 1976. It was used in the construction of the Museum at Grand Bend.

Rose Gardens Roller Rink gone but not forgotten

By KAREN PALMER
of The Observer

It has been 20 years since Dick and Elsie Rose closed the doors of Rose Gardens for the last time. The days when pop was a dime and hordes of kids spent Friday night roller skating may be gone, but many people still have fond memories.

Rose Gardens Roller Rink was purchased in 1951. It provided a place of recreation for young and old alike. The rink was run by Mr. and Mrs. Rose along with their daughter, Marilyn. The building may be gone, but it is still an important part of their lives.

Mr. and Mrs. Rose shared the responsibilities of operating the roller rink. "My wife ran the front

"THANK YOU!"
"ROSE GARDENS FANS"

"The Roses" wish to thank the hundreds of 'Well Wishers" who attended our Golden Wedding and Birthday Anniversary at The Holiday Inn on Sun., Jan. 16th, inspite of the frigid, inclement weather.

For the Many cards and other tributes on our behalf, we accept with thanks to you.

It is indeed, our honour and privilege to have befriended such great people in our time.

We especially appreciate the efforts of our family, Marilyn and Jack, Sheira and Brian, Adam and Jodi who planned and decorated

was understood that expansion would be difficult since the rink was built in a populated area. It was located on Sandy Lane west of Canatara Park, where apartment buildings now stand. When the need came to expand the rink, it was decided to close it since they could not get a permit for the addition because Rose Gardens was a non-conforming business in a residential area.

Rose Gardens closed on Oct. 14, 1974 with a final dance which over 2,000 people attended.

Although the roller rink was dismantled in 1974, the building lives on in the form of the Lambton Heritage Museum. The structural steel supports, roofing joists, and roof decking were donated to the museum, located from

104

Although the facility may be gone, memories of skating and dancing at the Rose Gardens are still vivid in many people's minds. Dick and Elsie regularly bump into former customers who are now grown adults themselves with children who echo the familiar phrase, "Our kids have nowhere to go like we did when we were their age." The Roses enjoy seeing the grown-up version of the kids who used to skate and dance. "It's rewarding to have so many friends who still care enough to say hello."

The building which housed Rose Gardens was later dismantled to make way for a high-rise apartment, but the structure lives on a few miles to the north. Dick and Elsie donated the structural steel supports, roofing joists and roof decking to the County of Lambton. It was resurrected on Highway 21 near Grand Bend, across from the Pinery Provincial Park and is now the main building of the Lambton Heritage Museum. The museum also houses some of the items used at Rose Gardens. An oak bench, originally from the old city hall and worn down even further by tired dancers taking a break at the rink, now sits in the museum. The smallest pair of rental roller skates is also on display.

Dick and Elsie recently visited their old building. "While at the museum I noted that they needed some cash drawers at the front door. We have such drawers left from Rose Gardens; they originally came from the old post office of Sarnia, torn down in the 1950's - every little bit helps out it seems."

The Last Dance

The end of the dance approaches. Depending on when and where you went dancing, the final number could be the orchestra's theme song, the country Home Waltz, or, in more recent years a frenzied explosion of sound through Marshall amplifiers, accompanied with a light show guaranteed to drive the crowd into an arm-waving mass of cheering humanity.

Do you remember the National Anthem being played at dances? It was usually God Save the King (or Queen); people actually stood at attention on the dance floor as the house lights were turned up, signifying the end of the dance and people made an orderly exit from the building. That tradition seemed to disappear in the late 50's or early 60's, and one of the rare occasions you hear the anthem played regularly today is at sporting events.

It's my hope that the young adults today who are able to dance in the few remaining pavilions in the province, appreciate the impact these halls had on so many lives. The good times that people are having today will be their special memories tomorrow, just as thousands of people before them have enjoyed the same experience. Whatever era you remember, or whatever music you enjoyed, the songs you grew up with - Big Band, country, or rock 'n' roll - the emotions you felt and the experiences you had were likely similar.

The decline of dance pavilions in Ontario has been slow but steady, particularly over the last 25 years. Some of the buildings have burned down (Port Elgin), others were demolished (Sauble Beach) and a few of the remaining halls have fortunately been saved and are being used for various purposes, such as Oliphant, Inverhuron and Kincardine.

Today it is difficult to imagine a dance pavilion operating six nights a week, and drawing large crowds every evening, but that was the norm in the 1930's and 40's. In terms of competition, there was very little else for people to do for entertainment. Look around the average home today and you'll see a television, VCR, stereo equipment and a computer with an Internet connection. A person is quite capable of amusing him or her self for lengthy periods without having to leave the home.

But not so long ago when people wanted to meet one another, what better place to socialize than at a dance? In many of the halls people arrived stag in groups, so there was a great opportunity to have a dance or two with someone, with no real pressure of having to stay with that person for the full evening.

By 1950 other forms of entertainment began to poke their heads into our spare time. Let's remember that leisure time and entertainment dollars are usually limited, so we must make the choice as to where we go for our amusement and where we'll lay down our cash. Gradually, dance pavilions began to feel the pinch of this competition.

As North America's love affair with the automobile increased, particularly after the War, the drive-in movie theatre business grew at a tremendous rate. In the United States alone, drive-in movies ballooned from 300 in the mid-1940's to over 5,000 in 1958. Probably the most severe impact on dance pavilions was the invention of television. Once The Box made its way into people's homes it completely changed our way of life. As the province loosened up some of the entertainment laws, sporting events became more popular than ever. The population became more mobile. The tire and gasoline rationing of WWII became a thing of the past. Automobiles were more reliable, the new highways could take you much further in a shorter period of time, so people simply started travelling and taking trips, rather than staying closer to home and taking in local entertainment.

As Big Band music gradually gave way to Rock, the transformation took many halls as casualties. This was not always the problem of the hall or the location, but sometimes due to the unwillingness of the owner to move with the times, especially if the owner was older and thinking about selling or retiring. Those who could see the change and decided to book in rock bands did very well as they catered to the huge bulge of the population born after the War. Many of Huron's pavilions had very prosperous years with rock music.

But ultimately, it was the lowering of the drinking age that really dealt a final blow to the pavilions in the early 1970's. Bars, which were formerly the hangout of travelling salesmen and older people, now became meeting places for the late teens and the early 20's crowd. Rock bands replaced lounge acts, small dance floors were built to accommodate those restless dancing feet and people loved it. They could buy a drink, see a band and dance. Pavilions could only offer the music and the dancing. Drinking sometimes took place in the pavilion parking lots, but that began to cause trouble in some towns.

By the late 1960's and early 70's, a new phenomenon began to take place, and that was the rock concert, largely an offshoot of Woodstock and Monterey Pop. Outdoor rock concerts, where people could take in as many as 15 bands over the period of a weekend, were staged all over Ontario. A pavilion could offer perhaps two bands at most in an evening, but could not compete with a weekend of camping and music.

By the late 1970's business for most of the remaining pavilions was terrible. Dancing was just **one** of many things to do for fun - not the **only** thing any more. The physical condition of many of these old wooden buildings was poor, necessitating significant upgrades just to preserve them. The decision was made by some owners to demolish the structure, such as in the case of the Sauble Pavilion while pavilions such as Port Elgin's burned to the ground.

This is not to say that dancing is dead. Far from it. People still like to get up and move, whether it is at a wedding reception, a company dinner/dance, or in a bar or dance club. Weekly dances are still held all over the province in

Legion halls, community halls and Masonic halls. Multi-purpose halls are still being constructed by private companies and community groups for banquets, craft shows and dances.

As people mature, their taste in music often expands. Big Band music is enjoying an unprecedented resurgence in popularity as a younger audience 'discovers' the excitement in this music form that was so prevalent 40 or 50 years ago. Ontario rock groups from the 1960's and 70's such as Little Caesar and the Consuls continue to re-unite and play gigs for people who come out to enjoy the songs they remember from 20 or 30 years ago. And then there are the troupers who have never stopped touring - Kim Mitchell, April Wine, Burton Cummings ...

So let's all agree that the music lives on! It's only the halls and pavilions that are relegated to memories in people's minds and pictures in this book. But it is sad in many ways to see a part of life which was so popular in this province gradually disappear, and the pavilions represented a major aspect of how we socialized during those years. They're gone now, and that's part of history.

Mac Beattie sums up his lament of the province's disappearing dance halls in the chorus of a song he wrote, "Deserted Dance Hall." Here are some of the lyrics:

Deserted Dance Hall
Copyright © Beattie Music Inc. 1982

Down the road - just out of town
Deserted now and tumble-down.
Just a memory of yesterday,
Memories of dancing feet
Where country folks would meet
And the oldtime bands
That used to play.

Chorus:
Deserted dance hall
Faded posters on your door.
Old faded posters - of the bands that play no more.

Photo Credits

Index

About The Author

Peter Young is a freelance writer and runs his own communications company. Between 1963 and 1975 he played keyboards (Hammond B-3 organ) with a number of Toronto-based rock bands and travelled extensively throughout southern Ontario, performing in many of the province's popular dance pavilions including some of Lake Huron's halls such as Kincardine, Port Elgin and Sauble Beach. He has recently completed a major research project covering every well known dance pavilion and dance hall in the Province of Ontario. Most of these wonderful pavilions have disappeared due to fire, demolition or conversion to other uses. Peter has delved into the unique past of each pavilion, interviewing owners or their descendants, employees, the general public and also many of the musicians who performed at the various locations.

His first book published in May 1997 - 'The Kee To Bala Is Dunn's Pavilion' - was received with great enthusiasm in Muskoka. The Kee continues to stage concerts featuring name bands.

Young's Lake Huron book, with its detailed text enhanced with many photographs and visual material, portrays a human interest slice of Ontario's social and cultural history from the 1920's to the present, with much emphasis on the Big Band period of the 1930's to the '50's, as well as the rock 'n' roll years of the 1960's and '70's.

"Come Dancing - A Celebration of Ontario's Dance Pavilions,"(© 1996 Peter Young) is being divided into regional texts similar to Lake Huron, so that the halls will all have sufficient space to be properly featured.

Thanks for supporting this project.

TO ORDER COPIES OF THIS BOOK:

Thanks for purchasing this book - We hope you enjoyed reading about the history of Lake Huron's Dance Pavilions and the significance they hold for so many people. If you would like to order additional copies as gifts for friends or relatives, please use this handy form below:

I would like to order _____ copies of **Lake Huron's Summer Dance Pavilions** @ $15.95 per copy plus $1.55 shipping and handling (Total $17.50). I have enclosed a cheque or money order made out to PDA Communications Ltd. for $_____

Please send this form to:
PDA Communications Ltd.
76 Hillcroft Street
Oshawa, Ontario L1G 2L2
Tel: Oshawa (905) 725-2954

Also Available from PDA Communications:

The Kee To Bala Is Dunn's Pavilion - by Peter Young
> The fascinating history of central Ontario's most celebrated dance hall is chronicled in detail, from its creation 70 years ago, to its present status as one of the province's premier concert venues. ($14.95 + $1.05 shipping - Total $16.00)